THE GRACED WOMAN

She is bold, confident, radiant, unique, highly favored, free, righteous, a woman of faith, and yes, she is...

THE GRACED WOMAN

a thirty-one-day devotional for women

Judith C. Matthews

ISBN-13: 9781530604395
ISBN-10: 1530604397

Foreword

The humble pleasure is all mine to recommend this work, which I believe to be of the Holy Spirit to all women who seek to begin the day with a definite direction of grace from our Lord Jesus Christ.

God's grace and forgiveness of sins (eternally—past, present, and future), which are encapsulated in the shed blood of Jesus Christ, as well as the freedom from condemnation and guilt, are emphasized throughout each section of this book. Those who read these contents will receive regular doses of the love of God and broken curses from their lives.

This is a long-overdue "manual," in a sense, that reflects the author's very graced life, and in some cases, sensitive and personal testimonies of faith and victory through Jesus Christ.

It is important for me to state that I know that while I was living out many of these personal examples of God's grace, I did not know they were benefits of God's grace entirely, at the time. This fact makes this book even more significant because many will come to the place of knowing more fully the power of Jesus's work at the cross, which exceeds the sometimes "well-known" fact of becoming free from eternal separation from God and also includes an exciting and enriching life while alive.

I admire the courage this book exemplifies in releasing many overcoming victories. Some of which are painful and could, without God's grace (which comes in the Person of Jesus Christ), otherwise have been fatal.

Watching and sharing life with this author, and serious student of the Word of God, as she has more than amply provided excellent nurturing as the mother of our three children, her qualification and calling to pen this writing rings truer than ever.

While Judith has focused these daily lessons toward women, after reading each of them, it is clear to me that all persons, regardless of gender, will benefit from this devotional.

One of the most difficult challenges most people face is where and how to begin their spiritual journey each day. In many respects, Satan, the enemy of success and progress, launches mental bombardments to prevent people from having the confidence that they are on the correct path for our Heavenly Father's loving and gracious blessings in and on their lives.

While reading the manuscript for this book, one particular scripture that continued to impact my thinking was Hebrews 10:22 (KJV): "Let us draw near with a true heart in full assurance of faith, having our hearts sprinkled from an evil conscience, and our bodies washed with pure water."

I believe this labor of love is metaphorically "pure water" that will be used greatly to deliver many who have suffered from "an evil conscience," not being convinced of God's love and Jesus's payment and consequent placement from the place of sin into His glorious kingdom. This is called "full assurance" of faith.

The Graced Woman will cause readers to supernaturally experience a "true heart in full assurance of faith" (in the finished work of Jesus).

Sola Gratia, (By His Grace Alone),
George M. Matthews II

Introduction

In a recent article published in *Business Insider* by Jacquelyn Smith, it was stated the way the first ten minutes of each day are managed will largely determine the productivity and effectiveness of the rest of the day. The first ten minutes can also set the tone, attitude, and mind-set for the day. Colossians 3:2 encourages us to set our minds and focus our attention on the things that are above, not on the things on the earth. We are to keep our mind-set on the higher things, the eternal treasures where Christ is, so that we can see things from His perspective. Whatever has your attention has your heart.

God wants to make your life better. Start your day off right! Spend a few minutes daily in the Word declaring who God says you are in Jesus.

Because of who Jesus is, not because of who you are, God declares that you are:

- Chosen
- Righteous
- His child
- Of a royal lineage
- Highly favored
- Valuable
- Healed
- Delivered
- Free

- Accepted in the beloved
- Prosperous
- Forgiven
- Loved
- Redeemed
- Restored
- Justified
- An overcomer
- God's masterpiece!

Now become who you are in Him today—*The Graced Woman*!

Grace: "God's overwhelming desire to treat us as if sin never happened."

— Kenneth Copeland

Day 1

Saved by Grace

"God saved you by His grace when you believed. And you can't take credit for this; it is a gift from God. Salvation is not a reward for the good thing we have done, so none of us can boast about it."

— *Ephesians 2:8–9 (NLT)*

Many years ago, I was relaxing in bed, and out of nowhere, the enemy began to show me my life. Within seconds, he took me through what appeared to be every mistake I had ever made, every wrong I had ever committed, and every failure I had ever experienced. I was overwhelmed, to say the least. During that encounter, he began bombarding my mind, telling me that I was not worthy of God's love, that there was no way I was saved, and that heaven would never be my eternal home. Tears began to stream down my face as I thought about the possibility of missing heaven. After all, I had done the best I knew to live for God. I loved God with all my heart. I had been raised in the church all of my life, sang in and directed choirs, and was at church whenever the doors were open. I knew no other life but "church life."

Fear gripped my heart at the thought of going to hell. I had heard too many stories about hell, and I knew for certain that was not the place for me. Satan continued to tell me I was not worthy. He continued to show me how I was not good enough and would never be good enough to make it to heaven. He began to ask me, "Are you sure you are saved? Do you feel saved? What if you haven't done enough to merit eternal life?" After years of serving God and "living right," I found myself still unsure of my salvation and where I would spend eternity.

I am so glad Ephesians 2:8 makes it very clear that there is not one thing we can do to merit salvation, nor is there anything we can do to contribute to our salvation. For by grace are ye saved through faith; and that not of yourselves: it is the gift of God.

The *Message Bible* makes this point even clearer:

> Saving is all His idea, and all His work. All we do is trust Him enough to let him do it. It's God's gift from start to finish! We don't play the major role. If we did, we'd probably go around bragging that we'd done the whole thing! No, we neither make nor save ourselves. God does both the making and saving (Eph. 2:8–9).

We are saved by grace alone, and we can take no credit for this; it is a gift from God. We are not saved by our own efforts. If we were saved by works, we could lose our salvation because if we stopped working, salvation would be lost. If we worked for salvation, we would also be able to share in the glory of salvation's benefits; however, this gift of salvation has nothing to do with our performance, nor is it based on whether we deserve it. If you did anything to earn or deserve salvation, it is not grace. I thought my service to God warranted salvation and right standing with God, but if God owed salvation to me for being a good person, or because I had done the best I could, that disqualifies salvation as a grace gift. We bring nothing to the table to deserve redemption, and any good works we perform are not the grounds of our status before God. Rather, they result from us having been chosen and receiving salvation as God's gift. It is His work alone. Romans 3:24 says we all are justified freely by His grace through the redemption that came by Jesus.

In Luke 23:39–43, Jesus hung and died on the cross between two thieves. One of the thieves cursed and mocked Jesus, but the other one, realizing that he deserved to die for his crimes, asked Jesus to remember him upon entering His Kingdom. Jesus paid this man's debt in full, and the thief, with no time to do anything but receive the gift, went to heaven that day.

In Luke 18:9–14, two men went to the temple to pray. One was a Pharisee, and the other a despised tax collector. The Pharisee began to pray by thanking God that he was not a sinner like everyone else. He did not cheat, sin, nor commit adultery. He fasted twice a week, and he was a tither. The tax collector, with his face in his hands, made a simple request: "O God, be merciful to me, for I am a sinner." In the end, Jesus declared, "I tell you, this sinner, not the Pharisee, returned home justified before God" (Luke 18:14, NLT). The Pharisee was not justified because his trust was not in God to save him; rather, his trust rested in the good works he did to try to save himself.

If God were fair, we would all be sentenced to hell, "For everyone has sinned; we all fall short of God's glorious standard. Yet God, with undeserved kindness, declares that we are righteous. He did this through Christ Jesus when He freed us from the penalty for our sins" (Rom. 3:23–24, NLT).

The grace that saves is the free, undeserved goodness and favor of God; He saves, not by the works of the law, but through faith in Christ Jesus. This free gift of God is not a purchase; it is a free gift, without money and without price. By this gift of salvation, we are no longer alienated from God. We can rest assured that through the blood of Jesus Christ, we are forever rescued from the wrath and judgment of God, and we are one with Him, just as He and Jesus are One.

"Thank God for this gift too wonderful for words!"

— 2 Corinthians 9:15 (NLT)

TODAY'S CONFESSION

Father, thank You that salvation is Your free gift to me. There is nothing I have done to merit salvation, and there is nothing I can do to earn salvation; it is completely free through Your grace alone. I give You all of the glory for this wonderful gift! Thank You for delivering me from bondage to sin and condemnation, transferring me into the Kingdom of Your beloved Son, and giving me eternal life. Thank You for sending Jesus to fulfill the law in its entirety for me.

I am a woman of grace. In Jesus's name, amen!

Ephesians 2:8, Colossians 1:13, Romans 6:23

Day 2

No Longer Condemned

> *"Therefore, there is now no condemnation for those who are in Christ Jesus, because through Christ Jesus the law of the Spirit who gives life has set you free from the law of sin and death."*
>
> — *Romans 8:1–2 (NIV)*

We are married to Christ! This union makes it impossible for God to condemn us. God no longer declares us to be wrong or unfit for use, nor are we doomed to punishment or forfeiture. Because we belong to Jesus, Romans 8:2 (*The Message*) states that we "no longer have to live under a continuous, low-lying black cloud. A new power is in operation." Grace gives us life and freedom. I encourage you to embrace what the Spirit is doing in us!

In 2 Corinthians 3:5–6 (NLT), we read, "It is not that we think we are qualified to do anything on our own. Our qualification comes from God. He has enabled us to be ministers of His new covenant. This is a covenant not of written laws, but of the Spirit. The old written covenant ends in death; but under the new covenant, the Spirit gives life." Verse nine of that chapter further states, "If the old way, which brings condemnation, was glorious, how much more glorious is the new way, which makes us right with God!" Condemnation kills, but grace through faith gives us His life upon our lives!

We can't earn our salvation, nor do we have to keep it. Jude 1:24 (*The Message*) says, "And now to Him who can keep you on your feet, standing tall in His bright presence, fresh and celebrating." The English Standard Version says God is able to "keep you from stumbling and to present you blameless before the presence of His glory with great joy." If we had to keep ourselves saved, we would be in a lot of trouble. Knowing this impossibility, God, Who saves us by His grace, also takes on the responsibility of keeping us saved and ensuring that we are kept to the end of all time. Not only does God take responsibility for keeping us saved, when the flesh wins out in some of the battles of life and we fall short, our Heavenly Father refuses to give up on us. Psalm 89:33 (NLT) states, "But I will never stop loving Him nor fail to keep my promise to Him." The *Message Bible* says in Psalm 89, "Yes, I'll stick with Him through thick and thin. No enemy will get the best of Him; no scoundrel will do Him in. I'll weed out all who oppose Him; I'll clean out all who hate Him. I'm with Him for good, and I'll love Him forever."

When God is on your side, you will win in life! No devil, no circumstance, no situation, no problem, and no test will get the best of you because God is with you for good, and He will love you forever! He loves us so much that even when you refuse to walk in the way He shows you, *The Message* Bible says, "But I'll never throw them out, never abandon or disown them." God is able to keep you saved because Jesus is continually interceding for you. Jesus is our High Priest, and the Bible says He understands our weaknesses because He was tempted with the same tests, but He did not sin (Heb. 4:15, NLT). Jesus, now in Heaven, is praying for believers.

But does this give us a license to go out and live it up, doing whatever we want to do? Unequivocally not! Our behavior does not make us righteous; however, God gives us power, His grace, to change and overcome bad habits—those areas where we habitually fall and make mistakes. We can't out-sin grace. Remember, God will never abandon or disown us. The more we sin, the stronger God's unmerited favor becomes. Sin cannot compete with God's grace. In the midst of sin, through the divine presence of the Holy Spirit, God will continue telling you what to do, then He will place in you the desire to do what He is telling you to do, and then He will give you the power to achieve His desire. That's grace. And "when it's sin versus grace, grace wins hands down" (Rom. 5:20, *The Message*).

TODAY'S CONFESSION

I declare and decree that I am in Christ Jesus; therefore, I am no longer condemned. A new power is in operation in my life. The spirit of life in Christ Jesus has freed me from the power of sin that leads to death. I am controlled by the Holy Spirit. I think about things that please the Spirit. I live in life and peace because my mind is controlled by the Holy Spirit.

God has taken up residence in my life, and I now live life on His terms. I decree today that I serve God, not in the old way of obeying the letter of the law; I am free to live a new life in the freedom of God. Absolutely nothing can get between me and the love of God that is revealed in Christ Jesus my Lord!

I am a woman of grace. In Jesus's name, so be it!

Romans 7:4–6 and 8:1–39

Day 3

Made in His Image

> *"So God created mankind in His own image, in the image of God He created them; male and female He created them."*
>
> — *Genesis 1:27 (NIV)*

I was so excited at the opportunity to be the first person among my siblings to ever fly on an aircraft! I was eleven years of age and proud to be a member of the school's safety patrol. At the end of the school year, the patrol team would fly to Washington, DC, to meet other safety-patrol teams throughout the United States and enjoy four days of sightseeing in the nation's capital. The passage of the Civil Rights Act of 1964 had just recently ended all state and local laws requiring segregation, paving the way for me to have the opportunity to attend this event.

Arriving in Washington, I quickly realized that I was the only African American female out of more than three hundred safety patrols, and there was only one African American male. I anxiously awaited my room assignment, and after receiving it, I joined the three Caucasian girls who would share the room with me. Upon arriving to our room, I overheard the three girls exchanging conversation about who would share the bed with the African American girl. No one wanted to sleep with me. No one wanted to be with me. No one wanted to share the bathroom I used or have any contact or conversation with me, solely because of the color of my skin.

My dream of this wonderful trip in DC was crushed. Those four days were four of the worst days of my life. I was talked about, ridiculed, and blatantly rejected. These young ladies saw me as inferior, and as less than the other safety patrols because of the way God had created me.

People sometimes miss the jewel you are because they judge your external appearance. They fail to recognize that before you were even formed in your mother's womb, God saw you and approved you (Jer. 1:5). Take a moment to think about that. You have received the stamp of approval from the Almighty God! Regardless of what people think, you are valuable to God. He didn't make you subpar, nor did He make you inadequate. He didn't make you inferior, regardless of the color of your skin or your physical makeup.

In 1 Peter 3:3–4, the Bible says, "Do not let your adorning be external, the braiding of hair and the putting on of gold jewelry, or the clothing you wear. But let your adorning be the hidden person of the heart with the imperishable beauty of a gentle and quiet spirit, which in God's sight is very precious." Your gift is too valuable to be judged merely by the external veneer. You are precious to God. People are not captivated by your outer appearance; they are captivated by your inner disposition. The word "precious" is defined as very valuable or important; too valuable or important to be wasted or used carelessly; greatly loved.

There are no ordinary people. There is nothing ordinary about you. God made you unique, and you are too valuable and important to God to be wasted or used carelessly. You are greatly loved by God, so much so that God says He keeps track of your every toss and turn through sleepless nights, He enters every one of your tears in His ledger, and He writes down every ache in His book (Ps. 56:8, *The Message*).

At the time of this publication, according to the world population clock, there are 7.3 billion people in the world. No two people have been found to have the same fingerprint. Fingerprints are even more unique than DNA, the genetic material in each of our cells. Although identical twins can share the same DNA—or at least most of it—they can't have the same fingerprints. Every believer is made in the image of God. We all have His DNA, yet He has uniquely given each of us our distinct identity.

Not only did He give us a distinct identity, Isaiah 43:2 says that God calls you by your name. You are not just a number, a symbol, or a statistic. You are the crown of God's creation. Our God even took the time to count every hair on your head! (Matt. 10:30).

You are a reflection of God's nature and His characteristics. By using both "image" and "likeness," God explained that He would create man to be just like Him. We not only look like God, we have the spiritual ability to understand His nature and learn to conform to it.

> And all of us, as with unveiled face, [because we] continued to behold [in the Word of God] as in a mirror the glory of the Lord, are constantly being transfigured into His *very own* image in ever increasing splendor *and* from one degree of glory to another; [for this comes] from the Lord [Who is] the Spirit (2 Cor. 3:18, *Amplified Bible*, Classic Edition).

You will never rise above the image you have of yourself. Begin seeing yourself today the way your Heavenly Father sees you—as the royal image of God Himself!

TODAY'S CONFESSION

Father, thank You for creating me in Your image and likeness. Thank You for approving me and accepting me. Thank You for loving me unconditionally. Thank You for making me unique, valuable, and precious to You. I declare today that Jesus lives in me. I am just like Him now! I possess the fullness of the Godhead in me now! Every time I look into the word of God, I see a reflection of who I truly am.

And as I behold Your Word, the more clearly I see and focus on Jesus, I declare that I am being transformed into Your very own image.

I am a woman of grace! Today, I go from one degree of glory to another.

Genesis 1:26–27, Jeremiah 1:5, 1 Peter 3:4, 2 Corinthians 3:18

Day 4

I Am Perfect in His Eyes

"Till we all come in the unity of the faith, and of the knowledge of the Son of God, unto a perfect man, unto the measure of the stature of the fullness of Christ."

— *Ephesians 4:13*

Have you ever heard the phrase "Nobody is perfect"? I am sure you have. It is a common phrase we use to excuse our shortcomings and failures. It gives us a reason to remain the same and never move toward change. By making that statement over and over, you allow this mental position to become rooted in your mind, and therefore you don't see yourself as perfect, or ever becoming perfect, nor do you see anyone else as perfect in Christ. This thought pattern may be the result of past failures, mistakes, hurts, poor choices, or a dissatisfaction with your current state in life. The Bible says in Proverbs 23:7, "As he thinketh in his heart, so is he." As long as these kinds of thoughts are allowed to bombard the heart, you are being robbed of the "you" God called into being before the foundation of the world.

I came across a statistic a while ago that said 30 percent of women (one in three) feel bad about themselves because they compare themselves to others. This process of comparison can lead to feelings of insecurity, inferiority, and low self-esteem. Another statistic reports that nine in ten women feel bad when they look in the mirror. One in three women feels anxious and hardly ever smiles back at herself. Many women have allowed these thoughts and poor self-images to cause them to waste the beauty, gifts, talents, and abilities God has placed within them. There are marketing campaigns designed to make women feel disparagingly about themselves in an effort to get women to purchase beauty-enhancement products. Such campaigns focus on making women feel as if they can avoid weight gain, signs of aging, and other unattractive qualities by simply purchasing and using the advertised products.

When people do not know who they are or who God has called them to be, they open themselves up to be who people, magazines, or ads say they are. By doing so, they are allowing the words of others, not those of our Heavenly Father, to affect the way they think, see things, and many times, who they become. The best "you" is an original that can never be duplicated. People need what "you" have to offer. There are situations in this complex world that "you" have been gifted by God to resolve. As far as God is concerned, you are complete in Him (Col. 2:10); you lack nothing, and you are entirely without fault or defect. Everything you need to be the best "you" already resided inside of you when you accepted Jesus into your life.

Hebrews 10:14 says that by that single offering, the sacrifice of Jesus, He performed everything that *forever* made perfect those who are made holy by His blood. Our High Priest offered Himself to God as a single sacrifice for our sins. *The Message* Bible says that "It was a perfect sacrifice by a perfect person to perfect some very imperfect people" (Heb. 10:12).

You may be imperfect on the outside, but Jesus, our High Priest, has forever made you perfect on the inside. As believers, we now live from the inside out. *Merriam-Webster* defines the word "perfect" as: being entirely without fault or defect—*flawless*; satisfying all requirements; faithfully reproducing the original; pure; total; complete; lacking no essential detail. As you go through the day today, see yourself without fault or defects. See yourself as flawless; you lack no essential detail. Philippians 2:5 says we have to allow this to become our mind-set. You must no longer see imperfections in yourself. Instead you must see yourself through the eyes of God, through the blood of Jesus. Deuteronomy 32:4 states, "His work is perfect."

TODAY'S CONFESSION

I am God's elected. I am chosen, royal, and special to God. He made all the delicate, inner parts of my body and knit me together in my mother's womb. He saw me complete and perfect in Him before I was born. Every day of my life has been recorded in His book. Before I even lived one day, He prepared every day of my life, and He made every one of them perfect. Thank you, Father, for making me so wonderfully complex! Your workmanship is marvelous—how well I know it. Thank You that I am the apple of Your eye, Your own special treasure. Thank You for forever making me perfect, flawless in Your eyes.

I am a woman of grace! In Jesus's name, amen.

Psalm 17:8; 139:13–14, and 140:16; 1 Peter 2:9; Romans 8:33; Deuteronomy 7:6

Day 5

I Am Highly Favored

> *"And he came to her and said, 'Hail, O favored one [endued with grace]! The Lord is with you! Blessed (favored of God) are you before all other women!'"*
>
> — *Luke 1:28, Amplified Bible*, Classic Edition

Imagine waking up to this greeting from your angel every day: "Good morning! You're beautiful with God's beauty, beautiful inside and out! God be with you!" (Luke 1:28, *The Message*).

What a way to start your day! But what did this mean for Mary? When God chose her to bear the Holy Son, I am sure she must have asked, "Why me? What is it about me that God has favored me above all other women?" After all, prior to this intervention, naturally speaking, there was nothing spectacular about Mary. She was a teenager, a normal girl of her day. There was nothing in her culture that made her stand out. She was born in Nazareth, a town of about fifteen hundred people. Her family is not even mentioned in the Bible; therefore, we know that she was not born into an elite or famous family in Bible history. Nathaniel even remarked about her town in John 1:46 (NIV), "Can anything good come from Nazareth?"

Being young, poor, and a female from a small town are all qualities that made Mary unsuitable in the eyes of people, yet God chose her to bring into the world the whole treasure of His grace. This is what makes God's grace so powerful: It's not about us, it is about Jesus! I am "grace-eligible" because of Jesus. Grace allows God to choose anyone to put greatness in, which means you and I are not excluded. Mary was favored, "endued with grace," by an act of God's will and plan. His grace alone placed her in this position to be used of God for the fulfillment of His plan for humanity. Mary did not receive God's grace because of her character; God looked at the quality of her trust and obedience in Him. He knew she would be willing, at all costs, to serve Him in possibly one of the most important callings ever given to a human being. Despite the fact that she would have to suffer disgrace as an unwed mother, and possibly be put to death by stoning, Mary was willing to step out in faith and trust in the words of the angel, "God is with you."

Joseph, of the Old Testament book of Genesis, gives us a great example of what it means to have "God with you." After being sold into slavery because of his brothers' jealousy of him, the Bible says in Genesis 39:2, "And the Lord was with Joseph, and he was a prosperous man." Though a slave, Joseph was "grace-eligible" because God was with him. God did not define Joseph's prosperity by his material possessions, where he lived, or where he worked. His success in life was defined by the fact that God was with him. Joseph's worldly master could see the favor of God on Joseph, and the Lord made all he did prosper in his hand. God blessed the home of Joseph's master, spreading favor over everything his master owned, at home and in the fields, until all his master had to concern himself with was eating three meals a day!

Even in the midst of great temptation, Joseph chose to risk his position of influence, be falsely accused, and then go to prison, rather than risk God not being with him. Even when people lie about or to you, do you wrong, abuse you, look over you, or forget about you—when the Lord is with you, you can expect God to work in you, by you, and for you. No one can stop God's favor on your life! As long as you think your job, education, or boss are the sources of your promotion and success in life, you miss out on the source of heaven's provision for you. You don't have to kiss up to people to get ahead. The Lord knows how to make you the head and not the tail. He knows how to take down one and put up another on your behalf to accomplish His will (Ps. 75:7).

Are you willing to accept God's plan for you, even when all you have is a Word from God? Will you step out in faith and do what God is leading you to do, even when you know it will cost you dearly? I am sure Mary and Joseph were fearful of the unknown; however, they did not allow their lack of understanding to cause them to doubt God. Their total dependence was on the grace or ability of God.

Today, you don't have to struggle for favor; it's God's gift to you as His child. You are "grace-eligible." God's grace promotes you. God's grace brings you before great men. God's grace makes your name great. Release God's grace in and on your life today by speaking forth God's Word in faith. On your way to work, say, "I am highly favored. God's favor surrounds me as with a shield" (Ps. 5:12). As you continue to speak God's favor over your life out of a revelation of Jesus's finished work, you will see more of His favor released in your life.

TODAY'S CONFESSION

I am blessed and highly favored! Thank You, Father, for Your favor that causes good things to happen in my life. Because of Jesus, I am "grace-eligible;" therefore, I fully expect the treatment that is afforded to those who are highly favored. I expect promotion and increase. I expect restoration of everything that has been stolen from me. I expect preferential treatment. I am graced for honor, recognition, and prominence. Through Your grace, things are made easy for me. Today You provide me with advantages, special privileges, and if necessary, policies and procedures changed for my benefit because I am special to you.

I am a woman of grace. In Jesus's name, amen!

Genesis 39, Luke 1:26–50

Day 6

God Loves Me Unconditionally

"To the praise of the glory of His grace, wherein He hath made us accepted in His Beloved."

— Ephesians 1:6 (KJV)

God loves you. He loves you without limitations or conditions. He has loved you with an everlasting love, a love that endures through all time. His love for you never fails, it never gives up, and it never runs out on you!

Although unnatural, it is more likely for a nursing mother to abandon her child than for God to abandon you. God will never abandon you. He will never forget you (Isa. 49:15–16). You are beautiful in God's eyes. He rejoices over you and makes no mention of your past sins, or even recalls them. He celebrates and sings because of you, and He refreshes your life with His love. He wants to show you how much He loves you and how happy He is with you. It doesn't matter how you feel about yourself; God loves you. He takes delight in you, and in His love, He gives you new life! (Zeph. 3:17, CEV, GNT, AMPC, ERV). As the Good Shepherd, He obligates Himself to see to it that you have no wants. He gives you the desires and secret petitions of your heart (Ps. 37:4, AMPC). How refreshing it is to know how much your Father loves you! He says in Zechariah 2:8 (NLT) that anyone who harms you harms His most precious possession. The New

International Version says that whoever touches you touches the apple of His eye. You are the apple of God's eye; He cherishes you above all others! When you accept how special you are to God, and all you are in Him, all negative thoughts about yourself will dissipate.

You are God's beloved—not because of what you do but because of what Christ did. God shows His love for you in that while you were still in sin, Christ died for you. He laid down His life for you. Before God laid earth's foundation, He had you in mind and settled on you as the focus of His love, to be made whole and holy by His love. Through His glorious grace, He adopted you into His family, and now you are "accepted in the Beloved" (Eph. 1:3–6). You may look at yourself and say, "There is nothing acceptable about me," but when God looks at you, He does not see you. God sees the One who never alters, He who is always the Beloved of God, always perfect, always without spot or wrinkle. Because He is well pleased with His Son, and you are in Him, God is well pleased with you, and you can never be "unaccepted" by Him!

You are eternally accepted by the Beloved, and it can never be reversed. You cannot be more accepted because of your worthiness, good behavior, or good works, nor can you be less accepted because of your failures. You don't have to measure up to a certain standard. There is nothing you can do to earn acceptance in the eyes of God; He accepts anyone who receives His Son by grace through faith. Regardless of what has happened in your life, if you have received salvation, you are still God's beloved because you are in Christ! Satan hates your knowledge of this truth. He knows that he has no power over you when you are conscious of the reality that you are God's beloved. You can walk in assurance and freedom when you know you are His beloved, and His love never changes toward you. You are liberated, able to be what He has designed you to be. Everything God demands of your life, you are now free to meet those demands in His power. Jesus now lives in you to live His life through you.

Webster's dictionary definition says that "to accept" means to receive willingly, to give admittance to, to regard with approval, to value, to esteem, to take pleasure in, or to receive favorably. How impactful it is to know that God, the Most High God, has accepted you willingly, favorably, with approval, value, and esteem, not because you merited His approval, but because Jesus, His Beloved, paid the price in full for your approval (John 19:30). Love is not something God chooses to do or give. Love is the very essence of God. He doesn't only love us; He *is* love (1 John 4:16). Love inspires His every action, guides His activities, and reflects His desires (1 John 4:10).

God accepts you. You belong to Him. "And as we live in God, our love grows more perfect. So we will not be afraid on the Day of Judgment, but we can face Him with confidence because we are like Christ here in this world" (1 John 4:17, NLT).

TODAY'S CONFESSION

Father, I thank You for the privilege of being called Your child and for loving me even as You love Your very own Son. Thank You for loving me unconditionally. Thank You for loving me with an everlasting, a never-failing love. Thank You for never, ever giving up on me. Thank You for my acceptance among the beloved. Although I am not accepted according to the measure of my prayers, my merits, my good works, or my faith, I thank You that I am accepted according to the measure of Your everlasting love for Jesus. And because I am in Him (Jesus), Your will for me is to enjoy every spiritual blessing that Christ enjoys in heavenly places. I am the apple of Your eye, and I receive Your unconditional love today.

I am a woman of grace. In Jesus's name, so be it!

1 John 3:1, John 17:23, Ephesians 1:3 and 6, Zechariah 2:8

Day 7

Grace to Forgive

"Be kind and helpful to one another, tenderhearted [compassionate, understanding], forgiving one another [readily and freely], just as God in Christ also forgave you."

— *Ephesians 4:32, Amplified Version*

Forgiveness is a choice we make each day when confronted with disappointments or mistreatments. It is not a feeling but a decision. During these times, you can make the choice to hold grudges and become bitter, or you can make the decision to forgive and become better. The choice is to be either forgiving or unforgiving. Forgiveness is not necessarily easy. Believe me, I know from personal experience that forgiveness is one of the most emotional and psychologically challenging experiences we will ever encounter. When you have been betrayed or hurt by those you trust, your natural response is to become angry, resentful, hostile, and bitter, and you are tempted to strike back or try to get even. At the same time, the emotional wounds from these kinds of situations can lead to sadness, and depression. In some cases, it leads to the destruction of lives. You know it is right to forgive, and you know it is what God has empowered us to do, but sometimes the pain can cause us to relive the wrong over and over again, constantly providing a connection back into a state of anger and resentment.

To forgive or cancel out wrong takes power. It takes more strength to forgive than to remain in offense. Thank God for His grace that empowers us to be able to forgive! Grace, God's power in us (Jesus living in us), enables us to forgive and live beyond our feelings. Whether you have been abused, neglected, victimized, or mistreated, you cannot afford to wait until your feelings change first. You must readily and freely forgive, *just as God in Christ has forgiven you* (notice that God's forgiveness proceeded our actions), regardless of how you feel. When you do, the grace of God to bring supernatural blessings is released into your life. However, if you choose to continue to live in unforgiveness, it will ruin relationships, leave you trapped in the past, and cause you to forfeit future healing and reconciliation offered to you through God's grace. Unforgiveness does not hurt the enemy; it hurts you and can potentially destroy your life. Not allowing grace to abound and bring about forgiveness causes a mere existence, not a life lived to the fullest.

You cannot undo what has been done. You cannot make right the wrong committed. You cannot "untell" a lie. You cannot undue rape or abuse. You cannot uncommit adultery. There is nothing you can do to change the past. However, by the grace of God, you can move forward and change the future. Your past is no indication of your future. No sin is beyond God's willingness and ability to forgive. If you committed a wrong, forgive yourself. God has already forgiven you and wiped your slate clean. He sees you clean through Jesus. If others wronged you, make the decision to let go of the hurt. Release those who have wronged you. As you show favor and kindness toward them, you cancel Satan's stronghold, closing the door to envy, strife, and every evil work, permitting God through His grace to completely set you free.

Forgiveness does not mean that you ignore, disregard, tolerate, overlook, or excuse the sins of others. It is not making allowances for a person's behavior; rather, it is a change of heart. When you allow God's grace to heal you, you may not forget the hurt. However, your heart will see the hurt differently. Grace allows us to see forgiveness through the eyes of Jesus and His finished work on Calvary.

Jesus's ministry was and is to forgive. Believers are encouraged in Luke 6 to love our enemies, do good to them, and be compassionate toward them. By doing so, we live out this God-created identity the way God lives toward us (Luke 6:35–36, *The Message*). Jesus also challenges us in Matthew 5:44 (*The Message*) to let people who hurt you bring out the best in you, not the worst. When someone gives you a hard time, you are to pray for them, and in doing so, you are acting as children of your Father in heaven. *Unforgiveness is not a shield or a defense; it is a thief and robber.* Don't allow it to rob you of the good life God has destined for you! Give yourself a gift—forgive your debtors. Allow God's overflowing grace to rule your heart and erase all hurt. As you do, the focus will shift from you to God, and you will begin to sense His grace, His unmerited favor, abounding in all areas of your life!

TODAY'S CONFESSION

Heavenly Father, thank You for forgiving me and for giving me the grace to forgive others.

Just as You are a forgiving God, gracious, compassionate, and slow to become angry, help me to daily practice forgiveness, compassion, and unfailing love toward others. Help me be slow to become angry. Today I get rid of all bitterness, rage, anger, harsh words, and slander, as well as all types of evil behavior. I live by faith and forgive by faith. I am not a criticizer. I do not find fault. I am forgiving. When people see me as a woman of Your grace, may they see that I am kind, helpful, tenderhearted, and understanding and that I readily and freely forgive.

I am a woman of grace. In Jesus's name, amen!

Nehemiah 9:17, Ephesians 4:31–32

Day 8

I Grow in Grace Daily

"But grow in the grace and knowledge of our Lord and Savior Jesus Christ. To Him be glory both now and forever! Amen."

— 2 Peter 3:18 (NIV)

All of the spiritual growth that occurs in our lives is by grace. Growth is a sign of life; without life, there can be no growth. If there is no growth after being born again, there is no life in the Spirit. Many believers have taken the first step to receiving Jesus as Lord; however, to possess all God has prepared for those who love Him, there must be growth in Him. Some believers are no more intimate with God after years of being believers than they were when they were first introduced to Him. They have not cultivated a friendship with God through daily prayer, devotion, and practicing His presence. Without contact, there can be no growth. Because growth is necessary for steadfastness, when the circumstances of life rear their heads, many believers are ill prepared and unable to persevere and advance in faith; therefore, they lead defeated lives, even though they have been saved.

A true sign that you are growing in grace is a progressive transformation into His likeness. As you spend time in the Word, you will begin to resemble Jesus; the grace that was in Him will transfer to you, and your behavior will begin to reflect His behavior. Your actions will begin to reflect His actions. Your thoughts will begin to reflect His thoughts. As you meditate on Jesus, your character will be refined, cultivated, and softened until it reflects His character. It is impossible to behold the Word of God consistently and remain the same. Paul says in 2 Corinthians 3 that when a person turns to the Lord, God removes the veil and the person is are face to face with Him. As you continue in His presence, you see that God is a living Spirit, and you find freedom in Him. You are liberated from the schemes of the enemy, and you are transformed into God's image. As God is allowed to influence your life more and more, you become like Him. The life of Jesus is on display in you, causing you to leave behind spiritual infancy—jealousy, revenge, squabbles, that which makes you look good or feel good, and being satisfied only when everything is going your way.

Grace does not grow in hearts that allow the flesh to rule. Evidence that you are growing in grace is that when Jesus becomes clearer, your faith grows exceedingly, hope abounds, love increases, and patience has full play so that you are complete, whole, and lacking in nothing.

We must labor to know Christ more clearly and more fully. The more you rely on God's grace, the more growth will manifest. In 1 Corinthians 15:10 (NLT), Paul says, "But whatever I am now, it is all because God poured out His special favor on me—and not without results. For I have worked harder than any of the other apostles; yet it was not I but God who was working through me by His grace." Paul, formally a persecutor of the church, understands what it means to grow in grace. Paul says that God's graciousness and generosity, not his hard work, are the causes of his growth. The change in his life was the result of God's grace. God alone is the Fountain of Life; He gives life, He nourishes life, and He increases life. By the grace of God, you are not what you are going to be. God is not finished with you yet! A new you is being evidenced every day. You are growing daily, through the good and bad. It took a lifetime for Simon, the son of Jonas, to grow into Peter; but it was done. And the very faults of his character became his strengths. If you will rely on God's grace, He will turn your misfortunes, mistakes, and mishaps into stepping stones toward His purpose and greatest good for your life!

God's gift of grace comes in many forms. I encourage you to use the grace you have, and grace will increase. Practice the truth you know, and many new things will become clearer. In 1 Peter 4:10 (Amplified), it says, "Just as each one of you has received a special gift [a spiritual talent, an ability graciously given by God], employ it in serving one another as [is appropriate for] good stewards of God's multifaceted grace [faithfully using the diverse, varied gifts, and abilities granted to Christians by God's unmerited favor]." God has blessed everyone, including you, with one or more of His many wonderful gifts to be used in the service of others. Use your gift well. Just as graces exercised are strengthened, graces unexercised will decay. The more grace grows, the more fruitful and productive you are to the Kingdom! "May God give you more and more grace and peace as you grow in your knowledge of God and Jesus our Lord" (2 Peter 1:2, NLT).

TODAY'S CONFESSION

All of the spiritual growth in my life is by the grace of God. I am what I am by the grace of God. All I can ever hope to be or have ever accomplished is by the grace of God. As I behold Your Word, thank You that my life is becoming brighter and more beautiful as I become more like You.

Father, thank You for my special gifts to the body of Christ. I understand that in whatever way I serve the church, I do so, recognizing that it is You, oh God, Who gives me the ability to do such. May You be glorified in everything I do through Jesus Christ. To You belong praise, glory, and honor forever.

I am a woman of grace. In Jesus's name, so be it!

2 Corinthians 3:16–18, 1 Peter 4:10

Day 9

I Am Restored

"And David enquired at the Lord, saying, Shall I pursue after this troop? Shall I overtake them? And He answered him, Pursue: for thou shalt surely overtake them, and without fail recover all."

— *1 Samuel 30:8*

In 1 Samuel 30, David discovers the richness of God's grace. Upon returning home to Ziklag, David and his men discovered that the Amalekites had raided Ziklag, burned it to the ground, and taken their wives, sons, and daughters as prisoners.

The people were deeply grieved. There was intensive weeping from these warriors. *The Message* Bible says they "wept and wept until they were exhausted with weeping." In the midst of such great loss, at a point when it seemed as though David was at his end, there was a turning point in his life. David "strengthened himself" in the Lord his God. Rather than choosing to allow grief, bitterness, and discouragement to conquer him, he chose to turn away from the problem and focus his attention on God.

All of us face difficulties in our lives, but we can have victory over them if we keep our eyes on the Lord. There was nothing about the circumstance that was encouraging, and if David had limited his focus to his present circumstance, he would have never seen God's ability to restore all things.

In such desperate times, we are often tempted to give up all hope, but we have a promise from God. In 1 Peter 5:10 (AMPC), we read that after you have suffered a little while, the God of all grace will Himself restore, confirm, strengthen, and establish you.

Some suffering is unjust; however, some of the suffering we experience is the result of poor choices we have made. Some people are reaping a negative harvest because of bad seeds sown. But thank God for His grace that forgives us of past, present, and future sins. Through God's undeserved, unmerited favor, we can experience glorious restoration in every area of our lives. God has promised to restore lost things because of wrong choices or any and all other misfortunes. God is able to restore the years that were lost to you and to cause the glory on your latter house (life) to be greater than that on your former house (earlier life). Whatever the enemy has tried to take away from you, God wants to restore. God will make it better than before; that's the kind of Father He is. Deuteronomy 30 says that God will exceed Himself in making things go well for you so that you can enjoy an all-around good life. God promises to restore everything you lost—not only that, He promises to pick up the pieces from all the places where they were scattered. He will reach to the depths of the earth to pick you up and bring you out. It matters not how far away you are; your God will get you out (Deut. 30:3–4).

While the world says that restoration is bringing something back to its original state, the biblical definition of restoration, or at least godly restoration, means bringing something into a state where it is even better than the original. When God says He will restore, He means He is going into your past to see the waste that has decayed and not only restore you, but bring you to a state that is better than before. God knows about the pains of the past. He has seen your struggles. He knows about the wasted dreams. He knows about the relationships that failed after much investment. He has seen your disappointments. He has seen the places where your hopes were destroyed! Today, just as in the past, Jesus restored sight, withered hand, and all other maladies through His blood at Calvary, He has also restored you. In 1 Samuel 30:18–19, God enabled David to recover everything the Amalekites had taken. David took everything back, including the flocks and herds of his enemies. In other words, he returned with more than he had lost.

Today, God turns the ashes of your past to beauty and a glory for your tomorrow. No matter how impossible your situation may seem in your eyes or anyone else's eyes, God has a plan to deliver you. God knows how to pick up the pieces and make something beautiful of your life. Do not look at the ashes. Do not look at what seems to have been lost. I declare to you by the Spirit of God that your time of divine restoration is now, in Jesus's name!

TODAY'S CONFESSION

Father, thank You for restoring my soul. You renew, revive, refresh, and sustain my life daily. You have quickened me, and through Your grace, You cause me to live.

Today, I am encouraged and filled with new joy. Thank you for giving back to me everything that was lost in my life. Thank You for restoring health to me and healing my wounds. Thank You for restoring my finances. Thank You for the double portion and everlasting joy. Thank You that godly relationships are restored in my life. Today, I decree that I recover all, and I will never be put to shame.

I am a woman of grace!

Psalm 23:3, Jeremiah 30:17, Isaiah 61:7, Joel 2:25–27

Day 10

His Grace Fully Meets My Needs

"Each time He said, 'My grace is all you need. My power works best in weakness.' So now I am glad to boast about my weaknesses, so that the power of Christ can work through me."

— 2 Corinthians 12:9 (NLT)

Three times, Paul, God's apostle of New Testament grace, sought the Lord that He might take adversity away from him. Three times, he asked God for a way out of his situation. Three times, he looked to God for a solution to his problem. And each time, God's reply was the same: "My grace is enough; it's all you need" (2 Corinthians 12:9, The Message). In essence, God is saying to Paul, "I am the grace; I am all you need."

All of us have faced adversity—hardships, persecutions, and calamities—at some point in our lives. Job 14:1 states, "Man that is born of a woman is of few days and full of trouble." Adversity has a way of pushing us beyond ourselves so that we can discover who God really is in us. Without times of adversity, we miss the opportunity to see God walk with us through the difficult times of life. It is during these life experiences that our human weakness opens the way for more of God's power and grace. His grace is always perfected in our weaknesses. His grace is manifested and magnified through human challenge.

The true measure of a person is how he or she ultimately deals with it when adversity crosses his or her path. There are some winds of change that blow into our lives that we cannot trample over, go under, or go around. If we want to experience God's grace in action, we must go through the desert of difficulty knowing that God's grace is sufficient. He is your grace, and He is all you need. It is during these seasons of life that we not only know God's name, we see His power. God is the only sufficient source of power that can come to our aid in every single situation. He does that by providing His grace.

In Exodus 14, as Moses and the children of Israel approached the Red Sea, the Bible says that God opened up a path "through" the water. With the Egyptians on one side and the Red Sea on the other, it looked as though there was no way out. Moses could have given up at that point. I am sure he looked at the massiveness of the sea, more than 190 miles wide, 1,200 miles long, and 8,200 feet deep. I am sure he considered Pharaoh's army, with 600 choice chariots, and all the other chariots of Egypt. Defeat appeared inevitable. If Moses had stopped at the Red Sea, he never would have seen the power of God divide the Red Sea and cause more than three million people to walk "through" it on dry land. The children of Israel had to go "though" adversity, but it was the catalyst to the Promised Land.

No matter what life's challenges may bring, always factor in God's abundant grace. Grace enables you to make it, no matter what the difficulty. It does not matter who turns against you, the obstacles you face, or even how many times you fail, God's grace is there to pick you up, revive lost hope, heal broken bones, and strengthen you in every weakness. Adversity is a given, but there is strength in overcoming. As Bishop T. D. Jakes says, "A setback is a setup for a comeback!" You can overcome anything by the grace of God!

Grace connects us to an inexhaustible place in God. His grace can never be depleted, nor is it ever inadequate. God's grace is always enough to meet the needs of any situation. When the apostle Paul received the revelation of God's grace, he said in verse 10 of 2 Corinthians 12, "Now

I take limitations in stride, and with good cheer, these limitations that cut me down to size—abuse, accidents, opposition, bad breaks—I just let Christ take over! And so the weaker I get, the stronger I become" (*The Message*).

Today you too may be overwhelmed with helplessness. You may be going through one of the lowest seasons of your life. Perhaps you have lost your job, or you are dealing with the loss of a loved one, or there may be relationship issues. Whatever you are experiencing today, please know that our Heavenly Father's grace is greater than any difficulty. His grace will fully meet the demands, needs, or expectations required to bring you to your wealthy place. God is your grace. He is all you need.

TODAY'S CONFESSION

Father, I thank You that Your grace is all I need. Your lovingkindness and mercy are more than enough, and they are always available for me, regardless of the situation. I refuse to focus on the difficulties in my life. Rather, in my weaknesses, I allow Your power to be perfected in me. I draw from Your strength today and am made strong. Help me to always trust You and rest fully in Your grace.

I am a woman of grace. In Jesus's name, so be it!

2 Corinthians 12:9–11

Day 11

I Know Who I Am

"But to all who believed Him and accepted Him, He gave the right to become children of God."

— *John 1:12*

I was born into a large family—four brothers and four sisters. Of the five girls, three had long, beautiful hair, and two of us had short hair. I always wanted long hair like my sisters. No matter what was done, my hair would not grow like my sisters' hair. One Christmas, while everyone received bicycles, Barbie dolls, and Easy-bake Ovens, my sister who had the shorter hair and I received what we thought were the greatest gifts from our parents: long-haired wigs. We were so excited! Back then, weave was not as prevalent as it is today, and wigs were not very popular, either. We put our wigs on and thought we were the most stylish girls ever! We could hardly sleep the night before school, in anticipation of going to school with our new look. Finally, we would be like our other sisters with long, beautiful hair. How wrong we were! As we skipped to the bus stop, excited to show off our new look, to our dismay, our friends laughed uncontrollably at us! By the end of the day, we were crushed, embarrassed, and too ashamed to ride back home on the bus.

Through the Word of God, I have come to know that the length of my hair does not define who I am. The family I was born into does not define who I am. How I look does not define who I am. My successes and my failures do not define me. What I drive, where I live, what I do, what I have or don't have does not define me. You can never use people or things as a personal point of reference.

Do not approach life from a flawed point of view. Don't measure yourself by the standards of others. Don't allow others to dictate how you perceive yourself and then make their perceptions of you your own. When the world defines you, it usually attempts to confine you. The moment you justify yourself by others, that is already an inferiority. Satan, the master of deception, wants you to be in search of and unsure of your identity. He knows that if he can get you to question your identity, you will forever question your destiny.

The only reliable source of our true identity is God. The Bible tells us, "If anyone is in Christ, He is a new creation" (2 Cor. 5:17). Through Jesus, you have a new identity! You have become a completely new person. Your old life, the old you with all of your inabilities, is gone, and a new life has begun! Jesus included everyone who believes in His death so that all who believe are included in His life—a far better life than you could ever live on your own.

Through Jesus, all of us are given a fresh start! In 1 John 3:1 (NLT), we read, "See how very much our Father loves us, for He calls us His children, and that is what we are! But the people who belong to this world don't recognize that we are God's children because they don't know Him." You are a child of the Creator of the universe! Don't be surprised that people don't recognize you. If they don't know Jesus, they may not recognize the new you, either.

God recreated you, loves you, and sent His son, Jesus Christ, to die for you. He is also the Holy Spirit Who transforms your life inside and out through His Word. The Holy Spirit heightens your possibilities. He transforms you into a new person by changing the way you think. When you allow Him to define your identity through the Word, you stand on a sure foundation for a life of peace and fulfillment. As you constantly look into the mirror of God's Word, you are able to maintain a consistent consciousness of your identity in Christ. The Word of God always tells you exactly who you are, what you look like from God's perspective, what belongs to you, and how you are to act as a daughter or son of God. The Word will also reveal to you any areas of your life that may not line up with God's Word.

You are defined by God and God alone. He has identified you as His own, and to ensure that you belong to Him, He sealed you by His Spirit. God stamped you with His eternal pledge, placing His Holy Spirit in your heart as a guarantee of everything He has promised to you (2 Cor. 1:22). To God be the glory for the great things He has done in you! Once and for all, you have been forgiven, declared innocent, exonerated of all wrong-doing, and made holy, and you are now the righteousness of God in Christ Jesus (Heb. 10:10). You are a child of God, and because you are His child, you are His heir and a joint heir with Jesus Christ. As you receive these truths, you will abandon any image of yourself that is not from God. You will stop accepting what others have said about you and how they have labeled you and defined you. You will stop looking for things that have already been purchased through the precious blood of Jesus. You will allow God's grace and peace to be poured into your life, bringing you into alignment with who you are in Him. You have already known the old you. Allow God, through Jesus, to reveal to you who you are in Him.

Jesus was able to face the incredible demands of His mission because He knew exactly who He was. He knew that He mattered to God, and that gave Him confidence to move with precision through life, accomplishing and fulfilling God's purpose. Your greatest treasure is within you. Understanding who you are in Christ Jesus will make a monumental change in every part of your life. Don't leave this world before people see the glory of Jesus in you!

TODAY'S CONFESSION

Father, I thank You that I am Your masterpiece. You have created me anew in Christ Jesus so that I can do the good things You planned for me. It is in You, Father, that I find out who I am and why I am alive. Before You made the world, You loved me and chose me in Christ to be holy and without fault in Your eyes. Thank You for taking me to the high places of blessing in You. Thank You for Your Holy Spirit as a reminder to me that I will receive everything You have planned for me, Your guarantee that I will receive the inheritance You promised to me.

Today I enter into the celebration of Your lavish gift giving by the hand of Your beloved Son, Jesus!

I am a woman of grace! Amen.

Ephesians 1:3–14 and 2:10

Day 12

Grace for Healing

"Many followed Him, and He healed them all."

— *Matthew 12:15 (NASB)*

It is the will of God that you are healed. It has always been the will of God that we are free from sickness and frailties. Our God is the same yesterday, today, and forevermore; therefore, healing is the will of God today. Nothing is impossible with God (Luke 1:37). There is no sickness or disease greater than the power and grace of God! Everything necessary for you to walk in divine health was completed when Jesus hung on the cross. His wounds became your healing (1 Pet. 2:24). Our part is to believe in the accomplishment of the finished work of Jesus. You must settle with finality the fact that God's will for you is divine healing and health. He has not put any form of sickness on you. He is not punishing you. He does not use sickness to humble you or teach you lessons. You don't have to wait on God; He has already sent His Word and healed you!

Healing comes totally because of the grace of God. Wherever Jesus went, He never made people sick. He healed them all, and in doing so, He always displayed the will of God. It was God Who anointed Jesus with the Holy Spirit and with power to go around doing good and healing all who were oppressed by the devil. Jesus was able to heal because God was with Him (Acts 10:38). Not only did Jesus heal, He authorized His disciples to do the same. In Acts 28, a chief official's father was ill with a fever. Paul went into the father's room, and when he laid hands on him and prayed, the man was healed. News of this healing spread throughout the island, and everyone on the island who was sick came and received healing from the Lord. God did not choose to leave some sick and heal others. He has the same love and compassion for you, and His desire for you is that you walk in healing and health.

In Matthew 9, Jesus was on His way to a synagogue leader's house to bring back to life his daughter, who had died very recently. On the way, He came in contact with a woman who had hemorrhaged for twelve years. She did not ask Jesus to lay hands on her. She did not plead and beg Jesus to heal her. She did not even try to get Jesus's attention. She didn't call her pastor. She didn't go on a fast. She didn't hold a prayer vigil. She wasn't "hoping and praying" for her healing. This woman decided that if she could just get to Jesus and touch His garment, she would be made well afterward. Jesus, realizing that virtue (God's grace to heal), flowed from Him, turned around and said, "Daughter, be encouraged! Your faith has made you well." And the woman was healed at that moment. Her faith in Jesus made her well.

By the time Jesus arrived at the home of the synagogue leader, they were already playing the funeral music. Knowing the power of His words, Jesus, in the midst of death, announced, "The girl isn't dead; she's only asleep." After putting the unbelieving crowd out, Jesus took the girl by the hand and pulled her to her feet—alive! Satan wants you to believe your situation is hopeless, helpless, and without the power to move, feel, or respond. He wants you to believe that there is no way out and that your situation is incapable of positively producing or functioning. But today, God sends His Word to heal you! Things around you are not dead, and you can use His Word and your faith to activate the dormant areas of your life to experience Jesus's joy and merriment.

In that same chapter, after Jesus left the synagogue leader's home, two blind men followed behind Him, crying out for mercy. They went into the house where Jesus was staying, and Jesus asked them, "Do you really believe I can do this?" I ask you the same question: "Do you believe Jesus's blood paid in full for every sickness and disease known to humans? Do you believe by His stripes you were healed? And if you were healed, do you believe you are healed right now?" The two blind men believed, and because of their belief, Jesus said to them, "Become what you believe." And it happened—they saw!

God's Word translation of Matthew 9:29 says, "What you have believed will be done for you!" Everything is possible for the person who believes. In Jesus Christ, there is enough grace to heal all, and it is by grace through faith in His finished work that you will see and become whatever you believe about Him. Every miracle is by grace. Galatians 3:5 (NLT) says, "I ask you again, does God give you the Holy Spirit and work miracles among you because you obey the law? Of course not! It is because you believe the message you heard about Christ." Every miracle that happens does so because of grace. God answers prayers because of His grace. Trust God to help you so that wherever there is doubt or unbelief, through His grace every trace of it may be taken away. Become what you believe! Allow your faith to lift you out of the sickness of sin into the health of righteousness.

TODAY'S CONFESSION

Father, I believe Jesus took my infirmities and bore my sicknesses, and by His wounds I have been healed. Jesus Himself bore my sins in His body on the cross so that I might die to sins and live for righteousness. I do not fear, for You are with me. I am not dismayed, for You are my God. Thank you for strengthening me, helping me, and upholding me with the right hand of Your righteousness. You are the Lord Who heals me and takes sickness from my midst.

Your Word is the final authority in my life. Not one word has failed of all of Your good promises. I conduct my life, family, finances, health, and everything that concerns me by Your Word.

Today I am a woman of grace, and I become what I believe!

1 Peter 2:24, Isaiah 41:10, Exodus 15:26 and 23:25, 1 Kings 8:56

Day 13

Grace to Persevere

"Brothers and sisters, I do not consider that I have made it my own yet; but one thing I do: forgetting what lies behind and reaching forward to what lies ahead. I press on toward the goal to win the [heavenly] prize of the upward call of God in Christ Jesus."

— *Philippians 3:13–14, Amplified Version*

His father died when he was six years old, forcing him to learn how to cook and take care of his siblings. He quit school in the sixth grade because he hated math. At age sixteen, he lied about his age and joined the army. In the 1920s, he sold tires and was the top salesperson in the state but got fired because of his temper. After several failed careers as a lawyer and a salesman of insurance, lamps, and tires, he found himself penniless. At the age of sixty-five, with little in terms of means at his disposal, he traveled door to door to houses and restaurants all over his local area. He wanted to partner with someone to help promote his chicken recipe. He started traveling by car to different restaurants and cooked his fried chicken on the spot for restaurant owners. Legend has it that Colonel Sanders, founder of the fast-food chicken restaurant Kentucky Fried Chicken, was turned down one-thousand and nine times before his chicken was accepted once! At the age when most people retire, Colonel Sanders built a global empire out of fried chicken, donating millions to charities, schools, and hospitals so that he would not be the "richest man in the cemetery."

What if Colonel Sanders had given up? What if he had thrown in the towel after the one-thousandth no? What if he had resigned after so many failed endeavors? The reason for his success is found in one word: perseverance—the ability to persist in an undertaking in spite of counterinfluences, opposition, difficulties, or discouragement. Whenever you feel opposition, pressure, challenges, and difficulty, know that it is a good indication that you are headed in the right direction. Continue to persevere. Satan does not fight people who are going the wrong way; he fights people who are headed toward the fullness of their destinies. He doesn't try to stop you from starting, but as you begin making progress, he presents opposition. I am so glad that the same God Who helps us start a task also supplies the grace—the power and the ability—to finish the work He has assigned to us. In persevering, remain confident that God, Who began a good work in you, will continue working in you until He completes what He started (Phil. 1:6). In the Kingdom of God, the way you finish is more important than the way you start. Sometimes we allow where we have been or where we are now to stifle where we are going. Ecclesiastes 7:8 (English Standard Version) states, "Better is the end of a thing than its beginning." God knows what He has put in you, and He knows your ending will be greater than your past! When you hit a "wall," it's not the end; it may be signaling that you are on the verge of a breakthrough. When you feel the worst, when failure is breathing down your neck, press in to the Word as never before, and declare, like Paul did in Acts 20:24, "But none of these things move me, neither count I my life dear unto myself, so that I might finish my course with joy, and the ministry, which I have received of the Lord Jesus, to testify the Gospel of the grace of God." God wants you to persevere so that you can tell others the good news about the wonderful grace of God.

Paul and Jesus never lost sight of their direction, and you too must not avoid losing sight of your destination. Hebrews 12:1–3 (*The Message*), tells us that Jesus, focused on the joy that was set before Him, put up with all kinds of things along the way: the cross, shame, and persecution were just a few. He persevered, beginning and finishing the race we are in, and now, He is in the place of honor, right alongside God. You are given grace, not only to endure, but to have joy along the way because you know that in the end, you win! You have a hidden treasure within you, and God withholds no good thing from His righteous seed (Ps. 84:11).

Stay the course. Don't let the past ruin your today. Forget what is behind as you press on and take hold of the things God has for you. You may have had an unfair past, but you don't have to have an unfair future. Leave the past behind as done with and settled. God's mercies are new every morning. If you will take God at His word, you can wake up every morning to a brand-new world. You can live life totally unhindered by the past. Paul says in Ephesians 3:8, "I have suffered the loss of all things and count them as rubbish, in order that I may gain Christ" (ESV).

I don't know the things that have happened, or what will befall you during the coming week, month, year, or even today. But God says you can be sure of this: His strength in you shall be equal to and surpass your day. God's strength will always be equivalent to your need. Whatever grace is necessary for you to make it through today—whether it is physical strength, wisdom, might, perseverance, direction, healing, influence—the Holy Spirit will see to it that God's grace is made available to you to meet your need and see you through to victory.

TODAY'S CONFESSION

Father, Thank You for the courage to let things go. I will not allow my past to ruin my today. I forget the former things; I will not dwell on the past. My eyes look straight ahead, and I fix my gaze directly before You. I choose to release the past through forgiveness and to focus on what is ahead of me.

This is a new day! The old has passed away, and the new has come! No matter what I face today or tomorrow, I walk in confidence, knowing that Your grace is equivalent to whatever I need. Today, I move into the good future You have prepared for me.

I am a woman of grace. In Jesus's name, amen!

Isaiah 43:19, Proverbs 4:25, Deuteronomy 33:25, Ephesians 3:8, 2 Corinthians 5:17

Day 14

I Live in His Peace

"And the peace of God, which surpasses all understanding, will guard your hearts and your minds in Christ Jesus."

— *Philippians 4:7, ESV*

It had been a normal morning for me as I prepared for work, said good-bye to my then-husband of less than two years, took my son to day care, and began my usually busy day at the office. I had been at work only for a little over two hours when I received a call that would drastically change my life. I was told that my father was waiting to see me in the lobby of the company where I was employed. As I arrived in the lobby and saw my father, I could tell from his demeanor that something was seriously wrong, but I was in no way prepared for what came next: "Your husband has been involved in a very serious accident at work, and you need to come with me to the hospital," my dad said. I tried to question him about what had happened and to find out the seriousness of the accident, but he avoided the conversation.

When we arrived at the hospital, I told the nurse who I was, and her expression instantly changed. She began to lead me to a small private waiting room. I began to cry and said, "Dad, I know what this means." The doctor came in and explained that my husband had been electrocuted at work and died instantly as the electrical current pierced his heart. At age twenty-two, I was a widow, left with a toddler who would never know his dad, and I was still more than a year from receiving my college degree. This was a defining moment in my life. I had to make a choice. I could have chosen to succumb to the pressure of what was ahead and been overcome with grief. I could have felt sorry for myself and had a "Why me?" pity party. I could have given up on my aspirations and dreams. Or I could accept God's comfort. In that moment, God offered me a peace that was beyond my understanding. In spite of the pain and sorrow, I chose God's peace, a comforting love, a sense of calmness, and a quietness that overrode every fear and anxiety. I chose His security in the midst of turmoil.

When God offers you peace, it does not mean you will not have trouble. It does not mean you will not have conflicts or challenges. Having God's peace means you will have His presence. Jesus tells us in John 16:33 that as long as you are in the world, you will experience difficulties; however, when you place your trust in Him, you can have unshakable peace knowing that Jesus has already deprived the world of its ability to harm you. There may be trouble all around you, but with God's peace, because you have set your mind at one with God and His Word, you can have calmness in the midst of the storm. The word "peace" (*shalom*) in Hebrew means completeness, soundness, health, safety, and provision. As you receive the peace God offers to you, regardless of the circumstances and situations of life, God's grace will arise in you, and you will find yourself in a state of harmony and well-being, without worry, because you trust God, and you know He will never leave you, nor will He ever forsake you.

Psalm 85:8 (NIV) says, "I will listen to what God the Lord says; He promises peace to His people…" When God makes a promise to you, you can expect it to be fulfilled because He is bound to His Word; therefore, it will come to pass. Psalm 29:11 says, "The Lord gives strength to His people; the Lord blesses His people with peace." You may not be able to stop the storms of life; however, you can control their *effects* on your life. The key to maintaining peace is found in Isaiah 26:3 (NLT): "You will keep in perfect peace all who trust in You, all whose thoughts are fixed on You." Peace is not making a decision in the midst of the storm; it is already knowing what you will do before the storm. Because you trust God, and your mind is set on God, when the storms of life come, His grace will empower you to be like the eagle and soar above them.

Seek God's peace, and pursue it today, for a future awaits those who seek peace. God promises us in Isaiah 54:10, "For the mountains may depart and the hills be removed, but My steadfast love shall not depart from you, and My covenant of peace shall not be removed..." God's love will never walk away from you, nor will His covenant commitment of peace fall apart. That same chapter promises in verse 14 that you will be built solid, grounded in righteousness, and you will live in peace. Jesus said, "I am leaving you with a gift—peace of mind and heart. And the peace I give is a gift the world cannot give. So don't be troubled or afraid" (John 14:27, NLT). The Lord of Peace Himself gives you peace at all times and in every way today! (2 Thess. 3:16, ESV).

TODAY'S CONFESSION

I pray that You, God, the source of hope, will fill me completely with joy and peace because I trust in You. Today I overflow with confident hope through the power of the Holy Spirit.

Thank You for Your gift of peace today at all times and in every way. I refuse to worry about anything; instead, I pray about everything. I tell You what I need, and I thank You for all You have done. And as I do this, I experience Your peace, which exceeds anything I can understand. I trust in You, Lord, without wavering, for Your Word declares that You are the eternal Rock. In You, Lord, I have a sure thing. I wait patiently for You to act. I refuse to worry about the situations that surround me. As my thoughts are focused and fixed on You, and my mind is focused on You, I am assured perfect peace. Thank You for everlasting strength and for Your covenant of peace today.

I am a woman of grace. In Jesus's name, amen!

Romans 15:13; Philippians 4:6–7; 2 Thessalonians 3:16

Day 15

I Am Redeemed

"You must know (recognize) that you were redeemed (ransomed) from the useless (fruitless) way of living inherited by tradition from [your] forefathers, not with corruptible things [such as] silver and gold, but [you were purchased] with the precious blood of Christ (the Messiah), like that of a [sacrificial] lamb without blemish or spot."

— *1 Peter 1:18–19 (AMPC)*

Jesus became sin for you—blameless, harmless, undefiled, and having done no wrong, He stood in your place so that you could stand in His place. He became a curse for you. He took your punishment. When you were still helpless, He died for you. Instead of leaving you captive to sin, poverty, and sickness, Jesus ransomed you by paying the ultimate price, the shedding of His innocent blood. God demonstrates His own love toward in that while you were yet a sinner, Christ died for you. Knowing your worst, God still came for you, forever confirming your worth in Jesus Christ. He paid a huge price for you. The Bible says in Isaiah 43:4 that He loved you so much that other noncovenant people were given in exchange for you. He traded their lives for yours—that's how much you mean to Him! *The Message* Bible says of that same verse, "I'd sell off the whole world to get you back, trade the creation just for you." You are valuable to

God, and He wants every one of His children who bear His name—every man, woman, and child whom He created for His glory.

Now that your ownership has changed, and concurrently, your status also changed, you don't have to suffer anymore. According to Galatians 3:13, you are free from the curse of the law! The word "curse" in Hebrew means devoted to damnation or destruction. The Greek word in the New Testament means the same thing—something doomed, devoted to destruction, and headed for judgment. Thank God you have been redeemed from the curse! You have been delivered from the hand of the enemy, and you now belong to God! Isaiah 43 says that He has called you by name (His own). When you go through the rivers of difficulty, you will not drown. When you are between a rock and a hard place, trust me, God is with you. When you walk through the fire of oppression, you will not be overwhelmed, for God is your personal Savior, and He will never forsake you.

Don't settle for living under the curse! God wants you to live an abundant, prosperous life, free from sickness, poverty, and spiritual death. Why live a life of doom and gloom when you have been redeemed from the curse of the law by the blood of Jesus Christ? The Bible says in 2 Corinthians 8:9 that He became poor so that through His poverty, you can become enriched, abundantly supplied. The Bible confirms this truth again in Galatians 3:14 (AMPC): "To the end that through [their receiving] Christ Jesus, the blessing [promised] to Abraham might come upon the Gentiles, so that we through faith might [all] receive [the realization of] the promise of the [Holy] Spirit." Jesus became sin for you so that you can now receive God's life, His Spirit! Under the New Covenant, Abraham's blessing belongs to you!"

Deuteronomy 28 declares that you are blessed when you come in and blessed when you go out. In other words, when God is orchestrating your life, you are blessed in everything you do! Your body is blessed. Your family is blessed. Your finances are blessed. The Lord has commanded the blessing upon you in your storehouses and in everything your hands touch! God desires the best for you. The blessing is on you! God longs to elevate you from your low estate to a high place of honor and promotion. Wherever you live, there is an anointing that comes with new ownership.

There is an anointing on you to get wealth! Don't settle for the crumbs that fall from the table. Don't listen to those who say you shouldn't desire material possessions in this life. God has blessed you so much that He has ordered His blessings to come on you and overtake you! It is unscriptural to believe God wants you to live in want, deficient of daily sustenance. Jesus shed His own blood so that you can live the abundant life! And you don't have to work for these blessings. They have been freely given to you through the blood of New Covenant. Don't try to figure out how God will manifest all He said He has done toward you. You are the seed of Abraham, and you have been blessed! Every place on which the sole of your foot shall tread, God has given to you! (Deut. 11:24).

Despite where you are today, stand on God's Word and claim the blessing of Abraham that is yours in Christ!

TODAY'S CONFESSION

Father, You alone are God. There is no other God. There never has been, nor will there ever be, another God. I am living evidence of Your greatness today! From eternity to eternity, You are God. No one can take anything from You. No one can undo what You have done. Thank You for the truth of redemption. Though I am completely unworthy of redemption, You redeemed me and filled me with Your grace and love. I declare that I am eternally redeemed. Thank You for allowing Jesus to take my place, to become sin for me, so that I might become the righteousness of God in Him. Thank You for purchasing my freedom. Today I declare that I am a woman of grace, and I receive the blessing of Abraham. Everything I set my hands to accomplish today is blessed! Everywhere I go today, I am blessed because of Jesus! Every enemy that rises up against me today is defeated before me, and people everywhere will know that I belong to You because of my blessed life.

I am a woman of grace. In Jesus's name, amen!

2 Corinthians 5:21, Galatians 3:13–14, Deuteronomy 28:2–10

Day 16

Graced for Greatness

"You have given him dominion over the works of Your hands; You have put all things under his feet."

— *Psalm 8:1*

Inside of you now is the person you are today. Simultaneously, existing on the inside of you is the person you could be. Last, and most powerful of all, on the inside of you is the person God has called you to be. You are carrying the spiritual blessing inside of you. You are walking around right now with everything you will ever need, a treasure—created by the power and ability of God—in an earthen vessel.

Now I want you to, for a moment, take a good, hard look at your life. Think it over, and then answer these questions: Who will you be tomorrow? Who will you be a year from now? Who will you be by the time you die? To go backward would be unwise because your past is not your potential. To remain the same may be easy and appear attractive, but to do so means you will digress rather than progress, resulting in no growth at all. If you want to reach your full potential, if you want to do something with this treasure you have, you will have to become like Abram in Genesis 12:1–2 (AMPC), where the Lord says to him, "Go for yourself [for your own advantage] away from your country, from your relatives and your father's house, to the land that I will show you. And I will make of you a great nation, and I will bless you [with abundant increase of favors] and make your name famous and distinguished, and you will be a blessing [dispensing good to others]." To the rest of the world, you may be a nobody, but to God, you are so valuable that He sent His only Son, Jesus, to not only set you free, but to forever position and empower you to do exploits for His Kingdom.

Seeds of greatness are in you! God desires to bless you with abundant increase of favors and make you distinguished, known by many because of His unmerited favor on your life. However, to get where God has ordained you to be may require that you break away from what is comfortable. It may require you to change your circle of friends. As God charts your course, it may require you to go into unfamiliar territory. You can also expect opposition. Paul described it in Romans 7:23 this way: "But I see in my members another waging war against the law of my mind and making captive to the law of sin that dwells in my members." Paul realized God had called him to greatness. Like Paul, you know God has a better life for you. You know God's Word says you are healed. You know He says you are above and not beneath. You know you are the head and not the tail. But there is a war internally—a different standard at work throughout the body.

The automatic pilot of our minds is trying to pull us back into a lower standard of thinking and living. God can never take you to the next level until you can get there through your belief system. Until you have an understanding of what exists on the inside of you, you will never walk in your full potential. No matter how many doors of opportunity open, you will never walk through them; you will talk yourself out of doing so by disbelief of your new identity. You will let destiny pass you, not knowing when you miss your appointment with destiny. God is not under obligation to reschedule that appointment.

The Bible says in Romans 8 that God knew you beforehand, and He destined from the beginning for you to be molded into the image of His Son, sharing His likeness. You are pregnant with potential! Not only did He know you beforehand, He called you by name—not your natural name, but you are called by your destiny—your predetermined purpose. As long as you are nameless (old nature), you have nothing to become; you are without a legitimate reason for your existence. When God spoke your new name, potential was birthed in you. When He called your name, provision and purpose were birthed in you. The power to become everything He called you has been released in you, and you lack nothing! Before anyone could skew your destiny, berate your purpose, or lower your value, God called you. And just as Satan came to Eve in the Garden of Eden and asked, "Did God really say…," he bombards your mind and asks, "Did God really call you to greatness? Do you really believe greatness is in you?" Know with assurance that, yes, God has called and chosen you for greatness. Whatever He has called you to do in life, He has equipped you with all that is necessary to accomplish the designated task. If supply never manifests, perhaps you don't need it to complete your assignment.

When God called you, at the same time He justified and acquitted you of all wrong. He has gifted you with right standing with Himself. God loves you so much that He did not stop at justification; He gave you His glory, raising you to a heavenly dignity and state of being.

In Mark 4, Jesus shares with us the parable of the mustard seed. He shows us how God can take an insignificant beginning and produce a great harvest. When we allow God's grace to saturate our lives, grace will take the smallest seed, the most unlikely individual, and bring about an astounding harvest. You may feel that your contribution is unimportant; however, God can use you to change the world. In the hands of God, you don't know what He might bring to pass through you!

God used one person, Moses, to lead more than three million Israelites out of Egypt. He used the woman at the well to save an entire town. He used Rahab, a harlot, to plan the protection and escape of Joshua's two spies. This same harlot married into one of the leading families of Israel and became an ancestor of Jesus. Don't discount the seed in you! God is able to do infinitely more, far above and beyond all that you can ask or think, according to the power that is active in you (Eph. 3:20).

TODAY'S CONFESSION

Father, I acknowledge all the good that is in me through Christ Jesus. Thank You for the Holy Spirit, my Personal Navigator, who lives on the inside of me to daily lead and guide me through life's obstacles, constantly pointing me to greatness. Thank You for making my name great. Thank You for blessing me with abundant increase of favors. Through Jesus, I am distinguished and worthy of respect of all with whom I come in contact. Thank You for blessing me to be a blessing. I decree that you have qualified me and equipped me with everything I need to fulfill my destiny, and I lack nothing.

I am a woman of grace, and I am destined for greatness! In Jesus's name, amen.

Genesis 12:1-3

Day 17

I Am a Reflection of God's Goodness

"And [Jerusalem] shall be to Me a name of joy, a praise, and a glory before all the nations of the earth that hear of all the good I do for it, and they shall fear and tremble because of all the good and all the peace, prosperity, security, and stability I provide for it."

— *Jeremiah 33:9 (AMPC)*

In my experience as a Baptist, there was an expression I heard regularly as the pastor would greet the congregation: "God is good all the time, and all the time God is good." I am not sure if we ever thought about the true magnitude of that expression. What it actually means is that it is impossible to have goodness without God. There is nothing about God that is not good. He is the very essence of goodness. His name means divine goodness. According to Genesis 1, everything He creates is a reflection of His goodness. Psalm 33:5 says, "The earth is full of the goodness of the Lord." God is entirely good! His greatness is indescribable. Psalm 145:3 says, "There are no boundaries to His greatness." Nothing can be added or taken away from Him to make Him better. Psalm 34:8 (*The Message*) proclaims, "Open your mouth and taste, open your eyes and see—how good God is. Blessed are you who run to Him."

It is out of this goodness that His grace flows through us, bringing peace, prosperity, security, and stability. David said in Psalm 27, "I had fainted, unless I had believed to see the goodness of the Lord in the land of the living." His goodness sustains us. His goodness protects us. It is out of His goodness that we receive divine favor and blessing so freely and lavishly bestowed on us. David says in Psalm 145:16 that God opens His hand and satisfies the desires of every living creature. Everything He does is right. When God speaks to you through the Holy Spirit, His sole purpose is to lead you to His highest good. You are the object of His affection. Let's look at a few scriptures that reflect the benefits of God's goodness to us:

> "Worship God if you want the best; worship opens doors to all His goodness."
>
> — Psalm 34:9, *The Message*

> "The goodness of God endureth continually."
>
> — Psalm 52:1 (KJV)

> "You crown the year with Your goodness, and richness overflows wherever you are."
>
> — Psalm 65:11 (GW. The ISV says, "You crown the year with your goodness; your footsteps drop prosperity behind them.")

> "For the Lord God is a sun and shield: the Lord will give grace and glory: no good thing will he withhold from them that walk uprightly."
>
> — Psalm 84:11 (KJV)

> "For You, O Lord, are good, and ready to forgive [our trespasses, sending them away, letting them go completely and forever]; and You are abundant in mercy and lovingkindness to all those who call upon You."
>
> — Psalm 86:5 (AMPC)

> "He wraps you in goodness—beauty eternal. He renews your youth—you're always young in His presence."
>
> — Psalm 103:5, *The Message*

> "And I will satiate the soul of the priests with fatness, and my people shall be satisfied with my goodness, saith the Lord."
>
> — Jeremiah 31:14 (KJV)

> "Every good and perfect gift is from above, coming down from the Father of the heavenly lights, who does not change like shifting shadows."
>
> — James 1:17 (NIV)

> "What a stack of blessing You have piled up for those who worship You, ready and waiting for all who run to You to escape an unkind world."
>
> — Psalm 31:19, *The Message*

Did you hear that? God has stacks of blessings piled up, ready and waiting on you! He withholds no good thing from you. Even when you fail, God is ready to forgive you and extend His mercy and lovingkindness toward you. Romans 2:4 (NKJV) says, "Or do you despise the riches of His goodness, forbearance, and longsuffering, not knowing that the goodness of God leads you to repentance?"

All that emanates from God is goodness. He is the foundation of goodness. Just as you want good for your children, as God's child, He wants only good for you. God's desires that you have no unmet needs, as a reflection that He is Jehovah Raah, the Lord your Shepherd, and He supplies all of your needs according to His riches in glory. He desires you healthy, as it reflects that He is Jehovah Rapha, the Lord Who is your Healer. He craves you living without fear so that you are a reflection of the truth that He is Jehovah Shalom, the Lord of Peace. As you go through the day today, allow your life to reflect His goodness, and others will be drawn to Him because of all the good, peace, prosperity, security, and stability He provides to you.

TODAY'S CONFESSION

How great is Your goodness, Father, and how great is Your beauty! You are infinitely and unchangeably good. The earth is full of Your goodness. Every good and perfect gift comes from You. Thank You for always satisfying me with Your goodness. My life is not empty but full of Your goodness because Christ is in me, the hope of glory. Every day I will praise You!

Today, I decree that You have crowned my year with goodness, and I lack nothing good. I will never stop praising You for Your goodness.

I am a woman of grace. In Jesus's name, amen!

Zechariah 9:17; Psalm 33:5, 34:1 and 10, and 65:11; James 1:17; Jeremiah 31:14; Colossians 1:27

Day 18

I Don't Frustrate God's Grace

"I do not frustrate the grace of God: for if righteousness come by the law, then Christ is dead in vain."

— *Galatians 2:21 (KJV)*

I can't tell you the number of times I was "born again." Growing up, I thought salvation was based on my ability to keep all of the commandments in the Word of God. I would get saved at a revival, but somewhere along the way, I would "miss the mark," and within the year, I would find myself back at the altar to be "born again" again because I no longer thought I was righteous. I counted on my good works to make me righteous; therefore, when I failed, I saw myself as no longer righteous in God's eyes.

What was I missing? A revelation of Titus 3:5 (AMP): "He saved us, not because of any works of righteousness that we have done, but because of His own compassion and mercy, by the cleansing of the new birth (spiritual transformation, regeneration) and renewing by the Holy Spirit."

The sole reason Jesus came into the world and suffered such a painful death was to pay the price for our sins and make us righteous forever before God. He did for us what we could never do for ourselves. Our salvation is secure, not on what we did through works or our own efforts, but by His grace. God cannot work in our lives when we reject His grace that has been freely given to us, by trying, through our own performance, to make ourselves righteous before God.

Galatians 3:21 says, "Is the law, therefore, opposed to the promises of God? Absolutely not! For if a law had been given that could impart life, then righteousness would certainly have come by the law." It is evidenced throughout the Bible that men have never found righteousness by the law. New life can come only through Jesus. He provides everything and requires nothing in return but ourselves, regardless of our condition. Righteousness happens only through total faith and dependence on Jesus.

Good works alone cannot save anyone. We are not made righteous by what we do, nor can we add anything to our faith to obtain right relationship with God. Romans 11:6 (AMP) says, "But if it is by grace [God's unmerited favor], it is no longer on the basis of works, otherwise grace is no longer grace [it would not be a gift but a reward for works]." If you and I had the ability to save ourselves, there would be no reason for Jesus's death; He would have died needlessly, without a cause. If we could be made righteous through the law, the *Holman Christian Standard Bible* says in Galatians 2:21, "Christ died for nothing." However, Galatians 2:16 (KJV) says, "Knowing that a man is not justified by the works of the law, but by the faith of Jesus Christ, even we have believed in Jesus Christ, that we might be justified by the faith of Christ, and not by the works of the law: for by the works of the law shall no flesh be justified." Our salvation is entirely dependent on Jesus's finished work at Calvary.

The Bible further solidifies that it is not our "good life" that saves us or condemns us. Being born again requires us to be born of the Spirit. Our works are jaded, but through Jesus, we are completely forgiven. Romans 5:9–11 (NLT) states, "And since we have been made right in God's sight by the blood of Christ, He will certainly save us from God's condemnation. For since our friendship with God was restored by the death of His Son while we were still His enemies, we will certainly be saved through the life of His Son. So now we can rejoice in our wonderful new relationship with God because our Lord Jesus Christ has made us friends of God."

God made you righteous! Stop struggling in your flesh. Freely receive what has been given to you through Jesus Christ. You have experienced the result of depending on yourself. Don't set aside or make void the grace of God. Allow Jesus to show you the results that are possible when you depend entirely on Him!

TODAY'S CONFESSION

Father, thank You that I am crucified with Christ. You have made me righteous through the blood of Jesus. Christ is living in me! I am not justified by my works, but by the faith of Jesus alone. I refuse to work or try to earn what has been freely given to me by grace. Christ did not die for me in vain. My days of trying and striving are over! I no longer depend on me; I entirely depend on You through the finished work of Jesus. Like the prodigal son of the bible who deserved nothing, I freely receive everything. Today, I expect the blessings of being your righteousness to manifest in my life.

I am a woman of grace. In Jesus's name, amen.

Galatians 2:20–21, 1 Corinthians 2:12

Day 19

I Am Delivered

"Many evils confront the [consistently] righteous, but the Lord delivers him out of them all."

— *Psalm 34:19*

Growing up as a PK (pastor's kid), church was a regular part of my weekly agenda. One message I remember hearing preached through the years is the story of Shadrach, Meshach, and Abednego from the book of Daniel. Much excitement would come as the many pastors talked about how these three Jews refused to bow down and worship the golden image setup by the king. According to the story, King Nebuchadnezzar issued a decree that whoever would not bow down and worship the golden image he constructed would immediately be cast into the midst of a burning, fiery furnace. Shadrach, Meshach, and Abednego, not being moved by the threat of death, refused to bow down and worship the king's idol. The king, infuriated by the Jews, commanded the furnace to be turned up seven times hotter than it was usually heated. The three men, bound, were thrown into the fiery furnace, fully clothed. But when the king looked into the fiery furnace, four men, not three, were walking around loose in the midst of the fire! God was with them.

Psalm 46:1 says, "God is our refuge and strength, a very present help in trouble." There is no plan that Satan can concoct from which God cannot deliver us. He is always present with a way out of any situation! *The Message* Bible says that God is "a safe place to hide, ready to help when we need Him." We can face the most extreme crises with confidence, knowing that God is present, ready to help us, ready to provide a way of escape. The fact that God is our refuge and strength does not protect us from trouble; however, we can rest assured that we do not need to be afraid. In 2 Kings 6:16 (HCSB), when surrounded by the Syrian army, Elisha said to his attendant, "Don't be afraid, for those who are with us outnumber those who are with them." Paul also reminds us in Romans 8:31–33 (*The Message*), "So what do you think? With God on our side like this, how can we lose? If God didn't hesitate to put everything on the line for us, embracing our condition and exposing Himself to the worst by sending His own Son, is there anything else He wouldn't gladly and freely do for us? And who would dare tangle with God by messing with one of God's chosen? Who would dare even to point a finger?" No problem is too big for our God!

Let's get back to our story about the three Jews who refused to worship Nebuchadnezzar's golden image. Daniel 3:27 states, "And the princes, governors, and captains, and the king's counselors, being gathered together, saw these men, upon whose bodies the fire had no power, nor was an hair of their head singed, neither were their coats changed, nor the smell of fire had passed on them." Did you notice the phrase "upon whose bodies the fire had no power"? Fire consumes. Fire destroys. Fire burns up. But fire has no power when it meets He who has all power! These men's hair, clothing, and every part of their bodies remained intact, even though the fire was seven times hotter than it was usually heated. Nothing was destroyed. Flames from the furnace killed the men who threw Shadrach, Meshach, and Abednego into the fire; however, the same fire was unable to harm these men because Jesus was present with them in the fire! The three men, although bound when they were thrown into the fire, walked around freely in the fire, completely unharmed!

The Bible says in Psalm 62:11 (AMPC), "God has spoken once, twice have I heard this: that power belongs to God." Jesus also says in Matthew

28:18–19 (AMP), "All authority (all power of absolute rule) in heaven and on earth has been given to Me…and lo, I am with you always [remaining with you perpetually—regardless of circumstance, and on every occasion], even to the end of the age."

Satan has been stripped of the power to harm you! God does not promise us a trouble-free life from Satan and his cohorts; however, rest assured that the "fourth man" is always present, and He is the same, yesterday, today, and forever! The same Jesus will walk with you through the fire, and you too will walk out of your circumstance completely unharmed!

TODAY'S CONFESSION

Father, thank You for being my safe refuge, a fortress protecting me from the reach of my enemies. I always find safety beneath Your wings. When trouble comes, I will remain still, unwavering in Your presence, and will wait patiently for You to act. You have promised that I will not be disgraced in hard times. Your Word also declares that You direct the steps of the godly, and You delight in every detail of our lives. Though I may stumble, I will never fall because You hold me by the hand.

Today I declare that I am courageous in the midst of every storm because I know that You are my refuge and strength, and You are always ready to help me through every dilemma. You dwell in me; therefore, I cannot be destroyed. You fight for me and protect me beginning at the very break of each day.

In Jesus's name, I am a woman of grace. Be it unto me according to Your Word!

Psalm 37:7; 46:1–11; and 61:3–4, 19, and 23

Day 20

Graced to Reign in Life

"Since by the one man's trespass, death reigned through that one man, how much more will those who receive the overflow of grace and the gift of righteousness reign in life through the one man, Jesus Christ."

— *Romans 5:17, Holman Christian Standard Bible*

Sinners are sinners, not because they sin, but because of one man's sin. Death reigned in every life because of Adam. Through all the generations from Adam to Moses, sin prevailed in the world with unquestioned dominion. Death had power over all mankind. But thanks be to God for His unspeakable free gift, Christ Himself! Through Jesus, believers have received overflowing grace and the gift of righteousness, which gives us the power to reign in life. We are righteous, not because of our righteousness, but because of one man's righteousness—Jesus Christ. Romans 5:19 says, "Because one man disobeyed God, many became sinners. But because one other person obeyed God, many will be made righteous." Verse 21 continues: "So just as sin ruled over all people and brought them to death, now God's wonderful grace rules instead, giving us right standing with God and resulting in eternal life through Jesus Christ our Lord."

To reign means to be king; to become powerful; to rule; to have dominion; and the authority to manage. Weymouth's New Testament translation of Romans 5:17 says, "Those who receive God's overflowing grace and gift of righteousness reign as kings in life through the one individual, Jesus Christ." You are the king of your life, and God has authorized you to manage your life based on His Word. You can rise from a life of mediocrity to a life that rules and reigns over sickness, poverty, negative circumstances, addictions, and any form of bondage. Being born again means more than securing a place in heaven. God has empowered believers through His overflowing grace to live like we are already in heaven! God wants believers to daily live in His grace, to be so filled that there is not enough room for anything or anyone more. He has freely given all of Himself, to give us everything we need to reign in life. Noted Bible theologian J. Vernon McGee said, "We recognize believers by their lives and not by their lips." God's abundance of grace is available to cause you to live a supernatural lifestyle, experiencing heaven on earth!

Genesis 1:26 (TLB) states, "Then God said, 'Let us make a man—someone like ourselves, to be the master of all life upon the earth and in the skies and in the seas.'" We were not created to be slaves or servants, but to be masters of all life. Who will you allow to master your life? Will death reign, or will righteousness reign? Will you master or be mastered in life? The Bible says in Galatians 4:3 that before Christ came, we were like slaves, ordered around with no say in the conduct of our lives. But God sent Jesus to buy back our freedom so that we are no longer slaves. We have been adopted as children of God, and as heirs, we run the world! Wherever God sends you, He expects you to rule. He expects you, through Jesus, to enforce His will on earth, just as it is in heaven. There is no sickness in heaven. There is no disease in heaven. There is no poverty or lack in heaven. No one is worried in heaven. There is no fear in heaven. Don't take on the nature of the world and live bound by the world's system when God has created you to rule, dominate, and govern this world (and everything in it).

According to Matthew 16:19, believers have been given the keys of the Kingdom of Heaven. We have power to bind and loose. Whatever we bind is bound, and whatever we loose is loosed. In the Old Testament, a trusted servant of the king wore the key to the king's house, and he could open or close the king's house. In Revelation 3, Jesus has the key of David, and He says in verse 7, "What He opens, no one can close; and what He closes, no one can open." Through the blood of Jesus, believers have been given access to God's house. In the natural world, when you have a key, you have permission from the owner to access his house whenever you want. You also have access to whatever he has in his house. When we receive His abundance of grace, and the gift of righteousness, God gives us access to His house and everything in it. As you walk in the authority of your identity in Christ, the manifestation of God's presence will begin to rule and reign in every area of your life, pushing demonic influences out. Sin and death will no longer reign. Everything on the earth that is out of alignment with the expressed will of God will come into proper order as His overflowing grace masters your life.

Romans 5:17 mentions "those who receive the overflow of grace and the gift of righteousness reign in life." God has freely given us His abundant grace and gift of righteousness; however, it is up to us to "receive" His gift. It is not necessary to work for these gifts, nor do you have to qualify for them. Become a receptacle of God's overflowing grace and gift of righteousness. Until you receive these gifts, you will live under the conditions of the law, a slave to the mandates of sickness, lack, poverty, fear, and the bondage of Satan. Instead of being ruled by Satan and all of his works, God's grace will cause you to rise up and rule and reign over him!

TODAY'S CONFESSION

I am no more sin-ruled; I am God-ruled! God's wonderful grace rules my life. Christ has brought me into this place of undeserved privilege where I now stand. I rejoice through problems and trials because I know that they help me develop endurance and strength of character, keeping me alert and sensitive for whatever God will do next in my life.

Today I rise up and receive God's overflowing abundance of grace and His free gift of righteousness so that I reign in this life! I boldly declare that Jesus is Lord of my life!

I am a woman of grace! Amen.

Romans 5:1–17

Day 21

Grace and Faith: God's Formula for the Good Life

> *"For it is by grace you have been saved, through faith—and this is not from yourselves; it is the gift of God—not by works, so that no one can boast."*
>
> — *Ephesians 2:8–9 (NIV)*

You were born to be blessed! You have a right to positively stand out in any crowd. Because of God's favor on your life, expect good opportunities today. Expect advantages in life. The blessed life is for you. God wants to give you the good life! The Creator of the Universe has put favor on you! You are radiating with His favor. God is for you, not against you. Today, recognize His goodness in your life that is made available by grace through faith.

God has anticipated every need you could ever have and has met those needs through the redeeming blood of Jesus. Before you ever had a financial crisis, God created the provision to amply supply every need. Before you ever had a problem, God foresaw it and provided a way of escape. Before you were plagued with illness, God sent His Word and healed you. Not because of who you are or what you have done, but through His grace, God has made these provisions available for anyone who will believe. Titus 2:11 (AMPC) says, "For the grace of God (His unmerited favor and blessing) has come forward (appeared) for the deliverance from sin and the eternal salvation for all mankind." Grace is made available to everyone, but not everyone receives God's grace. God's blessings and provisions are not in given response to who we are or what we have done. God met our needs through Jesus before we ever existed. Grace was already in operation before we ever came to be.

In Ephesians 2:8, the Bible shows us that grace and faith must work together for us to experience the good life God has prepared for us. God has a part, and we have a part in this grace relationship. Grace is God's part. It is the key element in His entire purpose. It is God demonstrating His love toward us. God gives us divine assistance, but not because we have earned it or deserve it. He puts His Spirit in our lives by grace, but not because He is obligated, compelled, or forced to do so. He extends grace to us, independent of us, because that is the way He has decided to be toward His children. We deserved His wrath, but He gives us His grace, which is better than we deserve, even though He owes us nothing.

Faith is our part. There must be a response to what God has done. Faith is our positive response to what God has already provided by His grace. It is our belief in what God has already done and then we receive what He has provided to us by grace. Evangelist Andrew Wommack simplifies this by saying, "Grace is what God does; faith is what we do." Grace is how God connects to us, and faith is how we connect to God. God doesn't need anything from us; however, we need everything from Him.

Faith does not induce God to move on our behalf. We can't make God do anything. You may have heard people say, "Let's bombard heaven with our prayers" or "Let's pray until we pray through," as if we can make God change His mind based on our actions. God does not need us to bombard heaven, nor is He moved by long, emotional prayers. He has already done the work. There is nothing left for God to do. Through faith, we accept what God has already done. Through faith, we take what is already real in the spiritual world and make it physical. When we have faith in God, appropriating what has already been done through His Word, the grace of God streams in with life and healing. Faith causes what is true in the spiritual realm to dominate what appears in the natural realm. In 2

Corinthians 5:7 (NLT), we read, "For we live by believing and not by seeing." Everything God does for us is accessed through faith.

Understanding the grace of God will release power in your life. Grace and faith are necessary to bring the power of God into manifestation. Grace alone does not get the job done; it has to be fused with your faith. You don't have to make something happen. Freely receive His grace, put your faith in what God has already done, and watch His supernatural power flow through you, releasing health, welfare, safety, preservation, and prosperity! It is by grace through faith that the promises of God become sure.

TODAY'S CONFESSION

I receive the good life! Father, I receive Your divine assistance at work in my life. By faith I appropriate all You have already done for me. I refuse to struggle, worry, or become frustrated trying to make something happen. I turn away from my own goodness. I look to Jesus and what He has done. I depend on the Holy Spirit to lead me into all truth, showing me what You want me to do. I declare today that resurrection power is in me! The power of the Holy Spirit is living in me; therefore, I live by believing and not by seeing. I thank You that through the Holy Spirit, You do exceedingly and abundantly above all I can ask or think according to the power of the Holy Spirit, Who is at work in me.

I am a woman of grace. In Jesus's name, amen!

Ephesians 2:8–9 and 3:20, 2 Corinthians 5:7

Day 22

I Rest in the Lord

"Come to Me, all you who labor and are heavy-laden and overburdened, and I will cause you to rest. [I will ease and relieve and refresh your souls.]"

— *Matthew 11:28 (AMPC)*

Do you need to be refreshed today? Do you need breathing room? Do you need relief from life's challenges? Are you burdened with the cares of this world? Just as it was with the children of Israel, Jesus invites you to come to Him and enter His rest.

"Rest" is defined as the ability to cease from exertion or motion; peace of mind and spirit; freedom from work, toil, strain, or activity. The mind is at rest when it ceases to be disturbed or agitated. Rest also means no longer striving to please the Lord with self-effort as far as your salvation is concerned. Rest is being settled, fixed, or secure. There is no more jostling in frustration from one thing to another. Receiving God's rest means that for the remainder of our lives and for all eternity we will lean on God, and in doing so, we are certain He will never fail to support us. We can depend on Him for and in everything.

According to Hebrews 4, God finished His part to ensure rest for every believer before the foundation of the world, and His promise of entering His rest still stands. On the seventh day of creation, God rested, not because He was tired or worn out; He rested because everything He created was completed perfectly. There will never be a need for Him to create anything again. The ability to procreate is in seed form and exists within everything God created (Gen. 1:11). The world was created to sustain itself, reproducing whatever is necessary to continue life.

Entering His rest, we share in all that belongs to Christ. However, we can miss the experience of entering His rest, resulting in continued struggles in life. If we fail to believe in the finished work of Jesus, we will never appropriate all that belongs to us. God invites us to rest from hard work, human effort, sweat, and tears, just as He rested after creating the world. We rest from the work of trying to earn our salvation, or qualifying for the Kingdom through self-effort. We look to Jesus, not ourselves, for our salvation.

When you become rest-conscious, you can get up every morning thanking God that He already has the answer to your prayers. No longer will you consider the circumstances; rather, you will focus on God's faithfulness to His Word. Rest in the Lord by focusing on the promise rather than the problems. Continually focus on what Jesus has done. Why? Because you know that with God, one touch of His favor can catapult you to a new level. One sudden shift can put you into overflow.

David writes in Psalm 110:1 (ESV), "Sit at My right hand, until I make your enemies your footstool." In the next verse, He says, "Rule in the midst of your enemies." *The Message* Bible says of that same verse, "Now rule, though surrounded by enemies!" These verses show us that we don't have to wait until problems are solved or situations are perfect before we rest. God offers us rest while He takes care of our enemies. By resting in Jesus's finished work, we will rule, even when it appears that we are surrounded by enemies. Our God ensures our victory by renewing our strength each day, from the "womb of the morning" (Ps. 110:3, NKJV). At the break of the day, God is there, offering fresh anointing, fresh wisdom, and fresh might!

In Isaiah 30:15 (NLT), God says, "Only in returning to Me and resting in Me will you be saved. In quietness and confidence is your strength." Our personal efforts to save ourselves will come to naught. Strength comes from settling down in complete confidence in God. Be diligent to enter His rest today!

TODAY'S CONFESSION

I trust in God, and I lean not on my own understanding. God is my source; therefore, I enter His rest. Before I ever had any needs, You, Father, anticipated every one of them and have already supplied every one of them. Before I ever came to this earth, Jesus died for me, bearing every sickness, pain, disease, weakness, and failure for me. He was beaten so that I could be whole and enjoy the good life. I am a woman of grace, and the power of God is on the inside of me now. I rest in the fact that You, Father, have completed everything for me perfectly. I rise up and use the authority given to me to speak to every situation in my life, knocking down every stronghold of the enemy!

I am a woman of grace. In Jesus's name, amen.

2 Corinthians 10:3–4; Hebrews 4:1–13; Proverbs 3:5–6

Day 23

I Am a Righteous Woman

> *"He made Him who knew no sin to be sin on our behalf, so that we might become the righteousness of God in Him."*
>
> — *2 Corinthians 5:21 (NASB)*

I had always heard about the "middle-child syndrome," but I never gave it much validity until the birth of my children. According to studies, in a family of three children, the middle-child syndrome starts when the middle child is squeezed between an older and a younger sibling, resulting in the middle child having trouble finding his or her niche in a family.

My oldest son was the "perfect child"—he always obeyed, achieved high marks in school, performed all of his chores, and never got into trouble. My daughter, the youngest child, has always been loving and caring and achieved high marks in school with very little effort, and she can win anyone over with her million-dollar smile. But such was not the case with my middle son. To give you an idea, I ran into the director of his preschool some twenty years after he had been a student, and the moment I told her who I was, she still remembered my son. It was not unusual to make several trips to every school he ever attended, from preschool to high school. Many people thought he would not accomplish much because of his past record; however, in every opportunity afforded to me, I continually told him who God created him to be. When others doubted his ability to succeed in college, I told him he had everything necessary already on the inside of him to attain his college degree. At every challenge, I reminded him of who he was in the realm of the Spirit, who God called him to be, (the righteousness of God in Christ Jesus). I knew that on the inside he was full of potential, a "born leader," influential, had a charismatic personality, and the list goes on!

Today, my middle son is a college graduate, born again, and serving as a director of youth ministry. When it comes to righteousness, many miss it because they measure their righteousness (right standing with God) based on their behavior. They are more sin-conscious than righteousness-conscious. They don't seem to understand that our spirits have been born again; however, our bodies have not been saved. The Bible says our own righteousness deeds are as filthy rags; therefore, our physical man has to be taught to obey the born-again spirit man. Our spiritual man is righteous, but our physical man still has the old nature of sin, and this sin consciousness will keep a believer in bondage, destroy faith, rob us of peace of mind, and make prayers ineffectual.

Author E. W. Kenyon made a profound statement: "Until man is righteous and knows it, Satan reigns over him. Sin and disease are his masters. But the instant he knows he is the righteousness of God in Christ, and knows what that righteousness means, Satan is defeated." As long as we remain sin-conscious, we miss perfect fellowship with the Father. We miss the benefit of having the life and nature of God dwelling on the inside of us. Even though the nature of God has been imparted to us, we continue to live a defeated, inferior lifestyle. When we grasp who we are in Christ Jesus, we will no longer act as if we are separated beings. As the righteousness of God, we will be bold as a lion (Prov. 28:1), standing in the presence of God without sin or inferiority.

Ephesians 4:24 (KJV) states, "And that ye put on the new man, which after God is created in righteousness and true holiness." The *Message Bible* says that when we put on this new man, we will "take on an entirely new way of life—a God-fashioned life, a life renewed from the inside and working itself into your conduct as God accurately reproduces His character in you."

Dare to take your place! God has made you righteous freely by His grace. All that was lost in the fall of Adam has been restored. Because you have been declared righteous, stand in the presence of our Father without sin consciousness or fear, and claim complete freedom. Everything in your past life has been wiped out, as though it never existed. You have been recreated—now function like Jesus and master Satan. Just as Jesus walked boldly in the world without a sense of inferiority of death, disease, and lack, you too can stand on the same ground and enjoy the freedom Jesus enjoyed in His earthly walk.

TODAY'S CONFESSION

I am a partaker of God's nature. Through the blood of Jesus, I am perfectly restored to fellowship with God. I am delivered from the dominion of darkness, and I have been translated into the Kingdom of God's dear Son. Satan's dominion over me is broken. I have been born into the family of God. I am the righteousness of God in Christ Jesus. I lose the sense of sin, and in its place I receive the sense of oneness and perfect fellowship with the Father. I repudiate every thought of weakness and sin consciousness.

I receive the nature of God in me. I am dead to sin, and I am alive unto God. Jesus has made unto me wisdom, righteousness, sanctification, and redemption.

In Jesus's name, I am a woman of grace! Amen.

John 1:16, Colossians 1:13, 1 Corinthians 1:30

Day 24

Bold as a Lion

"The wicked flee when no man pursues them, but the [uncompromisingly] righteous are bold as a lion."

— Proverbs 28:1 (AMPC)

What is it that will cause a young shepherd boy to refuse a bronze helmet and a sword when facing a giant standing more than nine feet tall, dressed in 126 pounds of armor, and carrying a sword with a tip that weighs more than fifteen pounds? What would possess a man to dig a trench around an altar, cut a bull into pieces, lay the pieces on wood, pour water on the wood three times until the wood, the sacrifice, and the trench are filled with water, and then command fire to consume everything? Better yet, why would a man (knowing the consequence of praying to God means that he will be thrown into a den of lions) kneel down as usual in his upstairs room, with his windows open, and continue to pray three times a day?

The answer is *boldness*. When believers understand they have been given the right to stand in the presence of God without guilt or inferiority, knowing that the blood of Jesus has justified and qualified them, they will become as bold as lions! They are not afraid of danger or difficult situations—not because of who they are, but because of Whose they are. Ephesians 3:12 states, "Because of Christ and our faith in Him, we can now come boldly and confidently into God's presence." Through Jesus

Christ, believers have an audience with God. We can approach Him with freedom, without restraint, fully confident that God has made every necessary supply of grace available to us.

As long as believers are sin-conscious, Satan holds them in bondage, robs them of faith in God, and their prayers become prayers of desperation, hoping for manifestation, rather than prayers of faith and undaunted confidence in the Word and ability of God. Sin makes cowards of men, but without a guilty conscience, the righteous have no need to run. In 1 John 3:21 (ESV), the Bible says, "Beloved, if our heart does not condemn us, we have confidence before God."

The righteous are fearless in difficult situations, knowing it is impossible for God to fail! When the opportunity to fear is present, the righteous override this spirit, speaking words of faith and prophesying their victory like Zerubbabel in Zechariah 4:7 (AMP): "What are you, O great mountain [of obstacles]? Before Zerubbabel [who will rebuild the temple] you will become a plain (insignificant)! And he will bring out the capstone [of the new temple] with loud shouts of 'Grace, grace to it!'"

The righteous are not intimidated in any way by the enemy (Phil. 1:28). They are not moved by their own stature or their physical appearance. Their boldness and confidence come through faith and trust in God's Word; therefore, they are free from uncertainty, and rather than prophesy a perilous fate, they prophesy a positive future.

In 1 Samuel 17, David considered not the forty days of threats from Goliath, nor did he consider his size, stature, or physical strength. He waxed bold, confident in God's ability alone, and declared, "You come to me with sword, spear, and javelin, but I come to you in the name of the Lord of Heaven's Armies—the God of the armies of Israel, whom you have defied. Today the Lord will conquer you, and I will kill you and cut off your head. And then I will give the dead bodies of your men to the birds and wild animals, and the whole world will know that there is a God in Israel! And everyone assembled here will know that the Lord rescues his people, but not with sword and spear. This is the Lord's battle, and He will give you to us!" (1 Samuel 17:45–47, NLT).

The righteous refuse to relent, even when it appears that they are outnumbered. They are courageous when faced with opposition. God declares in Leviticus 26:8 (NLT), "Five of you will chase a hundred, and a hundred of you will chase ten thousand! All your enemies will fall beneath your sword." Did you catch that? When believers join together, the power of God is intensified, and our enemies have no choice but to fall!

Don't allow fear to keep you from accomplishing God's purpose and plan for your life. Be bold as a lion! Step out in faith today knowing that God is with you wherever you go, and He will make every grace available to you to so that your victory is guaranteed!

TODAY'S CONFESSION

With boldness I enter Your presence, Father, because of Christ and my faith in Him, and I thank You that You make every grace available to me. I boldly declare that You are my light and my salvation; whom shall I fear? The Lord is the strength of my life; of whom shall I be afraid? In You, Father, I trust; I shall not be afraid. What can man do to me? I am strong and courageous. I am never frightened or dismayed, for You, Lord, are with me wherever I go. I do not fear bad news; I confidently trust the Lord to care for me.

With boldness and full confidence, I declare that my home is a safe dwelling and a quiet resting place because the power of God secures my life, my loved ones, and my belongings. I will never be seized with alarm nor struck with fear because it is my Father's good pleasure to give me the Kingdom!

Today I pray that You grant me the ability to speak Your Word with all boldness while You stretch out Your hand to heal, and signs and wonders are performed through the name of Your Holy Servant, Jesus.

I am a woman of grace, and I am bold as a lion! In Jesus's name, amen!

Psalm 27:1–4, 56:11, and 112:7; Joshua 1:9; Isaiah 32:18; Luke 12:32, Acts 4:29–30

Day 25

I Walk in Authority

"Behold, I give unto you power to tread on serpents and scorpions, and over all the power of the enemy: and nothing shall by any means hurt you."

— Luke 10:19 (KJV)

Have you ever heard a believer say, "I am waiting on God"? You may have used this expression yourself as you faced challenges or opposition from the enemy. If you have, I have great news for you: You don't have to wait on God anymore! According to Luke 10, Jesus has given you the authority to destroy all of the enemy's power, and when you walk in this authority, nothing will by any means hurt you!

In Acts 28, while Paul and other prisoners were being transported to Rome, they were involved in a shipwreck, causing them to take refuge on an island called Melita. As Paul gathered sticks to place on the fire they had built, a viper came out of the fire and latched onto Paul's hand. Those who saw the poisonous snake hanging on Paul's hand assumed he would begin to swell or fall dead suddenly, but Paul, knowing who he was in Christ Jesus, merely shook the snake off into the fire and "felt no harm" (Acts 28:5).

Paul did not react in fear when the viper latched onto him; he mastered the viper. He did not call on God or Jesus to help him deal with the viper. He did not wait to see what Jesus would do. Knowing the power of God in him, he (not Jesus) shook the viper off. Notice also that the Bible never says the viper bit Paul; it says the viper fastened on his hand. The viper, although latched on, was unable to infect Paul with its poison. Weapons may form against believers, but when you know who you are in Christ Jesus, the weapons are without power to prosper. Mark 16:18 (NLT) states, "They will be able to handle snakes with safety, and if they drink anything poisonous, it won't hurt them. They will be able to place their hands on the sick, and they will be healed." Don't go out and begin handling poisonous insects to test your power; however, if you come in contact with anything poisonous, in the name of Jesus, it will not by any means hurt you because you are divinely protected!

After looking at Paul for a while and seeing nothing happen, the onlookers began to say that Paul was a god. As a result of seeing the power of God in action in Paul's life, those who had diseases in the land were brought to Paul, and they were healed. What the enemy sends your way to bring harm, you can use the authority and power of God to turn it around for your good! Just as Paul walked in Kingdom authority and felt no ill effects from the viper, because we are in Christ Jesus, the same power and authority is in us! Believers are not powerless. The power to speak the Word of God in faith belongs to every believer, but it's up to us to use this power. In the strength of the grace of Christ, like Paul, believers are to shake off the temptations of Satan and suffer no harm. "The earnest (heartfelt, continued) prayer of a righteous man makes tremendous power available [dynamic in its working]" (James 5:16, AMPC). When a believer prays, something happens!

What you say and what you pray matters. One of Satan's strategies against believers it to convince them that their words don't matter. This is a great deception! The words a believer speaks reflects their outcome—not the devil or the circumstances surrounding them. You will never see anything in your life that hasn't first come out of your mouth. Everything you experience, both visible and invisible, was created out of words (Heb. 11:3). Every miracle Jesus performed was the result of words released from His mouth. He did not speak based on what He saw in the natural realm, He spoke from the spiritual realm, calling things that were not, as though they were, and He believed everything He said would come to pass. You are in Christ Jesus, and everything you need has already been finished! When you use His authority to speak according to the Word of God, and you believe, everything you say will also come to pass. Your words spoken in faith will bring what you need from the spirit realm into the natural realm, and no person or power can stop His Word from coming to pass in your life!

Our authority is expressed in words. According to Proverbs 18:21, the power of death and life is in the tongue. There are always two voices vying for authority: the voice of faith and the voice of fear (doubt and unbelief). When you speak, your words choose which authority will master your life. Power, the ability of God, is in His Word. When you believe and speak words in agreement with what God has already spoken, you release a force so powerful that everything in the universe has to adjust. If Jesus talked to a tree (Mark 11:11–14), and the tree obeyed Him, you too can speak to the situations in your life, and just like the tree, your situations must come into alignment with the Word and will of God!

We used to sing a song, "When we all get to heaven, what a day of rejoicing that will be. When we all see Jesus, we will sing and shout the victory." However, you don't need victory in heaven. There will be no battles to fight. You don't need authority in heaven; Satan won't be there, and sickness won't be there. *Now* is when we need victory. We need to take authority over poverty and lack, sickness and disease, and death now! Being able to defeat Satan in the earth now is the reason God sent Jesus to the cross. In Matthew 18:18, Jesus has given the authority to bind and loose to believers. Make the decision today to take the testimony of the Word rather than the senses around you. Don't accept anything that does not align with God's Word. Use the authority of Jesus, and change your world now!

TODAY'S CONFESSION

I am God's mouthpiece. Jesus is living His life in me. When I release His words, I release His power and presence in the earth. My voice gives the

Holy Spirit permission to bring God's will to pass in my life. Jesus has made me righteous, restored me to oneness with Him, and given me all authority in His name. I have a right to use the name of Jesus and expect what I say according to His will to come to pass. He has given me legal right, the power of attorney, to use His name. Whatever I ask, He gives to me. My words are His words. His words broke the power of death and demons and healed the sick, and they do the same things on my lips.

I am a woman of grace, and I exercise my rights now, in Jesus's name. Amen!

Luke 10:19; Matthew 18:18-20

Day 26

I Do Not Fear

"Fear thou not; for I am with thee: be not dismayed; for I am thy God: I will strengthen thee; yea, I will help thee; yea, I will uphold thee with the right hand of my righteousness."

— *Isaiah 41:10 (KJV)*

This scripture will always hold a special place in my heart, for it was the scripture that brought deliverance for me. I grew up most of my life without the assistance and guidance of my mother due to illness. I didn't know then what I know now—that Satan had robbed her of a productive life by plaguing her with mental illness. I witnessed firsthand the debilitating effects of a mental disorder and vowed that I would never deal with this condition, whether it was through stress, genetics, or any other reason.

The things that are familiar to us are the things Satan will sometimes use to buffet us. For example, if someone in your family is or was an alcoholic, the statistics say there is a good chance you will be an alcoholic too. If you lead a promiscuous life, chances are good that your daughter will also lead a promiscuous life. What you open the door to in your life affects you and everyone connected to you, although the full extent may not be readily apparent.

I experienced a very stressful period in my life several years ago, and as a result, Satan began showing me pictures of my life ending up just like my mother. I went from restful sleep to barely sleeping at all. I was living Deuteronomy 28:66–67 (NASB): "So your life shall hang in doubt before you; and you will be in dread night and day, and shall have no assurance of your life. In the morning you shall say, 'Would that it were evening!' And at evening you shall say, 'Would that it were morning!' because of the dread of your heart which you dread, and for the sight of your eyes which you will see."

One Sunday, while sitting in the morning service feeling as though I could no longer fight this battle, the Holy Spirit spoke to me and said, "Open your Bible." I picked up my Bible and opened it. The pages opened to Isaiah 41. From the pages of the Bible, God spoke to me: "Fear not, for I am with you; do not be dismayed, for I am your God. I will strengthen you. I will help you, and I will uphold you with My righteousness." As I continued to read, God said to me in verse 12, "Your enemies shall be as nothing, and a thing of the past."

Life came back to me! Joy came back to me! Peace came back to me! That day, I understood that the battle was not about what was going on in the natural realm; it was a spiritual battle, and fear was the root. Fear was the door I had allowed Satan to enter and then wreak havoc in my life. But there was no reason to fear, for God was and is with me! No longer would I be afraid of any form of illness because His righteousness had been imparted to me. Although this was a two-year ordeal of pulling down strongholds and bringing every thought captive to the Word of God, I could face life fearlessly because the God of omnipotence was on my side, and He that is in me is greater than any force around me!

Fear is the door Satan uses to connect you with every bad thing he wants to bring into your life, including generational curses. The Bible makes it clear this spirit is not of God, for it has torment (1 John 4:18) and leads to bondage. Romans 8:15 says, "For ye have not received the spirit of bondage again to fear; but ye have received the Spirit of adoption, whereby we cry, Abba, Father."

Fear cannot be tolerated on any level, for it will contaminate your faith. When believers do not know what the Word of God says, they fail to know the will of God, allowing Satan to use this ignorance to bombard the mind with thoughts of doubt, unbelief, failure, defeat, and destruction. Fear grows as you spend more time dwelling on what Satan says rather than what God has said. Satan is the accuser of the brethren. His ultimate goal is to get believers to think that what God has promised in His Word will not come to pass. Fear hinders the ability of God's promises to come to pass. Faith will not work when fear is present.

Don't open the door to fear! In 2 Timothy 1:7, the Word of God declares, "For God hath not given us the spirit of fear; but of power, and of love, and of a sound mind." Use the power of the Word of God, His unfailing love, and soundness of mind to drive fear and oppression far from you! When fear raises its ugly head, agree with David in Psalm 56:3–4, "What time I am afraid, I will trust in Thee. In God I will praise His Word, in God I have put my trust; I will not fear what flesh can do unto me."

TODAY'S CONFESSION

God has not given me a spirit of fear; therefore, I will never fear! God has given me power, love, and a sound mind. I refuse fear; instead, I receive the Spirit of adoption, whereby I cry, "Abba, Father!" Jesus is my help and my strength. I receive His perfect love for me. When fear arises, I put my trust in the finished work of Jesus, and I praise God for what He has promised. I yield no ground to Satan; I take back all that I have ever surrendered to him in the past through fear. I acknowledge that the Lord Jesus Christ is the Lord of all my life, and He is with me wherever I go. Even when I walk through the valley of the shadow of death, I fear no evil, for God is with me.

I am a woman of grace, and I walk fearlessly today. In Jesus's name, amen.

Isaiah 41:10–12 and 56:3, 1 John 4:18, Romans 8:15, Psalm 23:4, Joshua 1:9

Day 27

Graced to Master Emotions

> *"But none of these things move me, neither count I my life dear unto myself, so that I might finish my course with joy, and the ministry, which I have received of the Lord Jesus, to testify the Gospel of the grace of God."*
>
> — *Acts 20:24 (KJV)*

By nature, women are known to be emotional creatures. My husband says he believes there are at least six women on the inside of every woman. One minute we are happy and overjoyed; in the next few minutes, however, we may be crying and can't explain the reason, or depressed because of past hurts. Then in the next few minutes, we might be mad enough to hurt someone. But give us a few minutes, and we will be encouraging someone, telling them they can make it.

God created us to master life, and that includes our emotions. We are not victims who have no control over our impulses, desires, feelings, or emotions. We're not helpless. We can overcome depression, addiction, personality types, and any other negative feelings that try to move us in a certain direction. John 10:10 (NLT) says, "The thief's purpose is to steal and kill and destroy. My purpose is to give them a rich and satisfying life." The *Amplified Bible* says Jesus came that we might "have and enjoy life, and have it in abundance (to the fullest, till it overflows)." Satan, the thief, seeks to use your emotions to seize and carry away the rich, satisfied, abundant life Jesus has provided for every believer. He knows that emotions direct life. So what he seeks to do is gain control of your emotions and use them to steer you away from the will of God. Every time you get close to obtaining a promise from God, you can expect Satan to show up and attack your emotions so that he can get you off track. However, if you can begin to conquer your emotions, you can conquer anything and everything that comes in your life.

God created humans with emotions. The problem, however, comes when emotions dominate you and dictate your responses to life's challenges. Jesus was confronted with opportunities for negative emotions; but regardless of how He felt, He did not allow His emotions to rule. Just as you apply the Word for healing, promotion, and increase, you can apply the Word to negative feelings and take control of them.

In Acts 20, Paul begins to describe his journey in serving the Lord. In this passage, he expresses how he has done the Lord's work, but with many tears. He had laid his very life on the line, serving God no matter what. As he prepared to go to Jerusalem, the Holy Ghost warned him that hard times and imprisonment awaited him, but that didn't change his actions. Refusing to allow his emotions to rule him, Paul says in verse 24, "But none of these things move me." Paul had many opportunities to be overcome with emotions. Most certainly he could have become angry with the path his life had taken, even to the point of becoming angry with God. He could have been anxious about his upcoming journey to Jerusalem. But he allowed none of those things to move him. What mattered most to him was that he finished the work the Lord Jesus assigned him—the work of telling others about the grace of God! That is mastering emotions! And if Paul did it, so can you! Through Jesus, you have received grace upon grace. God has a better life, a better way chosen for you. Allow His grace to fill your heart and control every negative emotion.

Let's look at another passage in Proverbs 3:5–8 (NLT): "Lean on, trust in, and be confident in the Lord with all your heart and mind, and do not rely on your own insight or understanding. In all your ways know, recognize, and acknowledge Him, and He will direct and make straight and plain your paths. Be not wise in your own eyes; reverently fear and worship the Lord and turn [entirely] away from evil. It shall be health to your nerves and sinews, and marrow and moistening to your bones." As believers walk in dominion over anger, depression, anxiety, guilt, grief, eating disorders, and all forms of addiction, regardless of negative feelings, we can expect a healthy, long, and productive life! By turning away from negative thoughts and negative energy, and allowing God to direct our lives, we strengthen our emotional well-being. *The Message* Bible says in Proverbs 3:8, your physical body will glow with health, and your very bones will vibrate with life!

There will always be things that try your emotions; but you are now in Christ Jesus, and in Him, you have the power to change your response. You can do something about your emotions. You are not powerless; you can rise above every emotion and temptation! In Him, you have the ability to overcome everything life throws at you because the greater One is in you!

TODAY'S CONFESSION

I belong to God, and I overcome every negative emotion. Greater is He who is in me than he who is in the world. The Spirit in me is far stronger than anything in the world. I do not live according to how I feel on any given day. I am motivated by God's Spirit. I am led by the Holy Spirit, and I escape the erratic compulsions of a law-dominated existence. I am finished with frenzied and joyless grabs for happiness, uncontrollable addictions, envy, jealousy, quarreling, wild parties, sexual immorality, and comparing myself with others.

God never makes anything to fail! I allow the Holy Spirit to produce love, joy, peace, patience, kindness, goodness, faithfulness, gentleness, and self-control in my life, and against these things, there is no law that can bring a charge.

I am a woman of grace, and I am an original! So be it, in Jesus's name! Amen.

1 John 4:4, Galatians 5:20–24

Day 28

Born to Succeed

"She watches carefully all that goes on throughout her household and is never lazy."

— *Proverbs 31:27 (TLB)*

In his book *Signposts on the Road to Success*, E. W. Kenyon makes the following statements: "There is a gold mine hidden in every life. Nature never made a failure. Every man has success hidden in his soul. No one else can find it but himself. He holds the key to the hidden room. Failure comes because we never sought that hidden treasure. Failure comes because we tried to find it somewhere else. You can't find it anywhere else. Success, victory, and achievement are in you."

The message of grace reveals God's unearned, undeserved, unmerited favor toward us by allowing Jesus to become what we were so that we could become who He is. We can't work for this grace; however, every believer is expected to do business in the world's system based on God's Kingdom principles. Salvation is a free gift of God's grace, and nothing we do can purchase a special standing with Him. Nevertheless, the way we serve God and the testimony that our lives demonstrate to the world is very important to Jesus and His Kingdom.

You were born to succeed. Success, victory, and achievement are in every believer, and God expects us to do something with the abilities He has given us. In Isaiah 45:3 (NIV), God promises, "I will give you hidden treasures, riches stored in secret places, so that you may know that I am the Lord, the God of Israel, who summons you by name."

God desires that as believers, we are always abounding, always excelling, always experiencing promotion in life, not just for the purpose of living large, but so that we can promote His glory and advance His kingdom. In 1 Corinthians 3:9 (AMPC), it says we are "fellow workmen (joint promoters, laborers together) with and for God." We have a part to play in our success. We hold the key to the "hidden room," and as we yield to the Holy Spirit, He is able to reveal to us all of the innermost parts of our being (Prov. 20:27).

Success, victory, and achievement are in every believer, but a spirit of laziness will keep believers from achieving God's best. In Matthew 25, Jesus uses the parable of the talents to reveal to us that laziness is without excuse in the Kingdom. It matters not what gifts, talents, and abilities we have been given; what matters is what we do with those gifts, talents, and abilities. Ecclesiastes 9:10 says, "Whatsoever thy hand findeth to do, do it with thy might; for there is no work, nor device, nor knowledge, nor wisdom, in the grave, whither thou goest."

In the parable of the talents, when the master returned, two of the three servants increased what was entrusted to them, and as a result, they were promoted. However, the servant to whom the least was given allowed fear to cause him to waste his abilities. The master accepted no excuse for a lack of increase. The obstacles the servants faced didn't matter; the master expected increase from each of them. The servant who did nothing was not condemned for not producing as much as the other servants; he was condemned for not doing anything; not even making an effort. Jesus called this servant wicked, slothful, and unprofitable. The word "slothful" comes from the Greek word *okneros*, which means lazy or idle. Jesus was displeased with this servant because he had a do-nothing, lethargic, lackadaisical, apathetic, lukewarm attitude toward life.

In Revelation 3:15–16, Jesus shows us His position on lukewarm believers: "I know thy works, that thou art neither cold nor hot: I would thou wert cold or hot. So then because thou art lukewarm, and neither cold nor hot,

I will spue thee out of My mouth." Lukewarm believers are those who maintain a "middle-of-the-road" position. They have no fervor or passion and a lazy attitude that keeps them from maximizing their potential. Although success, victory, and achievements are in them, they never use the Word of God to develop these seeds and thus remain unprofitable and useless for the Kingdom. Full of God's ability and purpose, yet never realizing their value, believers who remain in a lukewarm state contribute nothing to life. Their gifts, talents, and abilities go with them to the grave.

Are you giving God your best in your church, on your job, in your home, and toward your spouse? Are you using the gifts, talents, and abilities God has entrusted to you to promulgate the Gospel of Jesus? Can God count on you to increase what has been given to you, or when He returns, will He find your treasures hidden?

If you have gotten off track, use these scriptures to help you renew your passion for your assignment(s):

> "Work hard and become a leader; be lazy and never succeed."
>
> — Proverbs 12:24 (TLB)

> Lazy people want much but get little, while the diligent are prospering."
>
> — Proverbs 13:4 (TLB)

> "In everything you do, put God first, and He will direct you and crown your efforts with success."
>
> — Proverbs 15:22 (TLB)

> "Do you know a hard-working man? He shall be successful and stand before kings."
>
> — Proverbs 22:29 (TLB)

> "And not because we think we can do anything of lasting value by ourselves. Our only power and success comes from God."
>
> — 2 Corinthians 3:5 (TLB)

"And whatsoever ye do in word or deed, do all in the name of the Lord Jesus, giving thanks to God and the Father by Him."

— Colossians 3:17 (KJV)

TODAY'S CONFESSION

Because the Lord is my Shepherd, I do not want for anything. I am daily loaded with benefits. I receive all things that pertain to life and godliness. God is my Source. He is my only Source. God uses any resource He chooses to accomplish His will for my life. Great grace is upon my life. There is no lack of anything in this earth for me. I have all things richly to enjoy.

In everything I do, I put God first, and He directs and crowns my efforts with success. I denounce a lazy spirit. I will never be an unprofitable servant. I do not associate with idle, gossiping people; I associate with winners. The glory of God is upon my life. His power is in my life. I am built up and secure.

I am a woman of grace. In Jesus's name, amen!

Psalm 23:1 and 103:1–5, Acts 4:33, 1 Timothy 6:17, Proverbs 15:22

Day 29

Built on Faith, Grace, and Hope: A Threefold Cord Not Easily Broken

> *"Through Him also we have [our] access (entrance, introduction) by faith into this grace (state of God's favor) in which we [firmly and safely] stand. And let us rejoice and exult in our hope of experiencing and enjoying the glory of God."*
>
> — *Romans 5:2 (AMPC)*

How privileged we are as believers to have access to God, our Father! Through our Lord Jesus Christ, we can enter this treasure house of grace without shame, guilt, or condemnation. Using the access card of faith—knowing that Jesus is the Son of God—we can firmly and safely stand fearlessly in the presence of God and receive all of the blessings promised in the Word.

How does this process start? With a little four-letter word, "hope." There have been times in my life when the only thing that has kept me from sinking is hope. The temptation to throw in the towel, give up, and quit was there, but hope pushed me to new expectations. When everything around me said there was no reason to believe that the promise would take place, hope kept me focused until faith brought manifestation.

Hebrews 6:11–12 (NIV) says, "We want each of you to show this same diligence to the very end, so that what you hope for may be fully realized. We do not want you to become lazy, but to imitate those who through faith and patience inherit what has been promised." Hope is the ingredient that causes you to keep at it with committed faith until you receive all that is promised.

Abraham experienced this hope in the fight of faith for the birth of his son, Isaac. Romans 4:17–18 (NLT) says, "That is what the scriptures mean when God told him, 'I have made you the father of many nations.' This happened because Abraham believed in the God who brings the dead back to life and who creates new things out of nothing. Even when there was no reason for hope, Abraham kept hoping—believing that he would become the father of many nations. For God had said to him, 'That's how many descendants you will have!'" *The Message* Bible says in verse 18, "Abraham believed anyway, deciding to live not on the basis of what he saw he couldn't do but on what God said He would do." Abraham refused to consider his age (at the time, he was one hundred years old), Sarah's age, nor his impotence and Sarah's aging womb. What are the odds of having a child after so many years of infertility? Yet Abraham refused to believe his situation was hopeless. He never wavered in faith, being fully convinced that God is able to do what He promises (Rom. 4:20–21).

Abraham shows us that hope does not disappoint. Hope will not put you to shame. Hope does not leave you empty. The grace of hope never fails because the love of God is shed abroad in your heart by the Holy Spirit (Rom. 5:5). The grace of hope does not depend on your love or on your obedience to God; this hope is based solely on God's undeserved, unearned, and infinite love poured out to you.

Hope requires a reason for its possibility, which means that a promise for the desire must be found in the Word of God. Without the knowledge of God's will and promise, there can be no hope. And when hope has no foundation, it is reduced to wishful thinking. Without hope, God has nothing of which faith can make a reality.

We see hope and faith working together in Hebrews 11:1 (AMPC): "Now faith is the assurance (the confirmation, the title deed) of the things [we] hope for, being the proof of things [we] do not see and the conviction of their reality [faith perceiving as real fact what is not revealed to the senses]." When hope has no foundation, it is just wishful thinking. But when hope has a reason for its possibility, if we diligently persevere like Abraham, hope will turn to faith, and faith will bring everything hoped for into reality.

E. W. Kenyon said it best: "Hope is faith in seed form, and faith is hope in final form." Hope starts the walk of faith, believing what God has promised will come to pass someday. Faith, on the other hand, is believing you have it now. Hope allows you to first know what you *can* have, and faith allows you to know what you *do* have. Hope says it is possible, but faith guarantees manifestation. Once the full assurance of God's will comes alive in you, hope begins to build the foundation of faith. As you act on faith, the faith of God connects to the grace of God, releasing His ability in your life. And when that happens, whatever you are believing to manifest, wait patiently, as it is sure to come to pass. God's Word guarantees it!

TODAY'S CONFESSION

I walk by faith and not by sight! I am not moved by what I see, nor am I moved by what I feel, nor am I moved by what others say. My hope is built on Jesus's finished work, and by faith, I patiently wait for the manifested promise. Just as Abraham trusted God to do what only He could do, I trust that God has already done what He said He would do. My situation is not hopeless. Whatever I am facing today is not without hope. I believe the One who brought Jesus to life when conditions were hopeless will also bring to life any situation in my life that appears hopeless. Even when it seems there is no reason for hope, I will keep hoping because I know my hope will turn into faith, and faith guarantees manifestation!

I receive manifestation now! In Jesus's name, I am full of hope and faith. I am a woman of grace! Amen.

Romans 4:17–25, 2 Corinthians 5:7

Day 30

Heir of God's Glory

"And now that you belong to Christ, you are the true children of Abraham. You are His heirs, and God's promise to Abraham belongs to you."

— *Galatians 3:29 (NLT)*

You are in the family of God, a blood relative of Jesus, and that makes you an heir of all things! Not only an heir, you are a joint heir to a great inheritance in Christ Jesus. According to Galatians 3:13–14, you have been freed, released, bought back from poverty through Jesus Christ, and now you are an heir to Him who owns and operates the universe!

In Galatians 4:4–7 (NIV), the Bible says, "But when the right time came, God sent His Son, born of a woman, subject to the law. God sent Him to buy freedom for us who were slaves to the law, so that He could adopt us as His very own children. And because we are His children, God has sent the Spirit of His Son into our hearts, prompting us to call out, 'Abba, Father.' Now you are no longer a slave but God's own child. And since you are His child, God has made you His heir."

You are God's own child, a truth that is unalterable! Through Jesus, you have been adopted into the royal family of God, and you have legal access to Him as a daughter, not a slave. Because Jesus has been appointed heir of all things (Heb. 1:2) and you are a joint heir with Him, all of God's promises—all of the blessings of grace, glory, and righteousness—belong to you. The Blessing of Abraham is yours!

What is "The Blessing of Abraham"? Everything you will ever need: health and healing, victory, dominion in every area of life, abundance, and the power to be a blessing to all the families of the earth (Gen. 12:1–3). When "The Blessing" is in operation, nothing and no one can stop you or hold you back from obtaining everything God has promised.

What makes The Blessing even better is the fact that it is not conditionally based on our actions. We don't have to work for this inheritance. There is nothing any believer can do to earn "The Blessing"—it's a gift from God, inherited by every believer from the new birth. The moment you were born again, you inherited all things! In 1 Peter 1:4 (EXB), it says, "Now we hope for [or this new birth provides us with] the blessings God has for his children [an inheritance]. These blessings [or This inheritance], which cannot be destroyed or be spoiled [corrupted; defiled] or lose their beauty, are [is] kept in heaven for you."

We are heirs of everything in God's Kingdom. Because we are His heirs, why do we ask God for healing? Why do we ask God for faith? Why do we ask Him for provision? Why do we ask for what we already have? Ephesians 1:3 (GW) says, "Through Christ, God has blessed us with every spiritual blessing that heaven has to offer." In 2 Peter 3:4, it says, "Since the fathers fell asleep, all things continue as they were from the beginning of the creation." Take a moment to comprehend that verse. God has already provided every spiritual blessing heaven has to offer, and they are being kept right now for you in heaven.

You might be saying, "I don't need spiritual blessings in heaven. I need them here right now!" Paul prays in Philemon 1:6, "That the communication of thy faith may become effectual by the acknowledging of every good thing which is in you in Christ Jesus." The more a believer acknowledges every good thing in him or her in Christ Jesus, faith increases. And as faith increases, believers will experience heaven on earth! All that God has provided for you will manifest in the earth as you exercise your faith.

If you want change, make a change! You can't keep talking lack and experience "The Blessing." Receive the best life you could ever live. Start developing an inner image of your inheritance by acknowledging all of the good that is in you in Christ! Take your rightful place as a daughter or son in God's family, and accept your full inheritance now!

TODAY'S CONFESSION

I am in the family of God. I am Abraham's famous descendant, which makes me an heir according to the covenant promises. I am an heir of God! I am developing an "heir of God" mentality. I am richer than I ever dreamed! I receive all of the good things God has for me. The blessing of God makes me rich and adds no sorrow. I keep out of debt, and I owe no man anything but to love one another. I receive abundance, increase, and no lack in any area of my life now!

Today I decree that I am no longer a servant; I am a daughter of God. I have been born again into the royal family, the richest family ever known! I have a priceless inheritance. My Father owns everything, and He has provided all things for me. Jesus became the curse for me, releasing me from the curse of poverty and giving me the privilege of sharing this vast inheritance with Him. I live in the blessing now!

I receive my inheritance in Jesus's name! I am the graced woman! Amen.

Galatians 3:13–14 and 29, Romans 13:8

Day 31

The Graced Woman

"There are many fine women in the world, but you are the best of them all!"

— *Proverbs 31:28 (TLB)*

She is bold, beautiful, confident, radiant, unique, and highly favored. She is priceless, far more precious than the finest jewels. As a matter of fact, Jesus sees her worth as so valuable that it cannot be estimated by any material object. The value He put on her is so great that He had no reservation in paying off every debt with His very life!

Nearly everyone likes to look at beautiful objects; however, true beauty cannot be measured by something as shallow as external factors. Beauty has deceived many. Don't misunderstand me —outward appearance is important, but external beauty may not last. Physical bodies can deteriorate. External beauty can be insufficient, fade, and come to nothing. Inner beauty, on the other hand, can never be destroyed or limited.

The graced woman has much more to offer! From the very beginning, the graced woman was made with purpose. Everything necessary to fulfill her purpose and complete her destiny was put in her by God Himself; consequently, only her Maker defines her true purpose and determines her worth. He fashioned and formed her to ensure that she had no needs or lacked anything. She is equipped to meet any need. Her strength is not in her arms and hands. This virtuous woman is virile without being masculine. Though the weaker vessel, her strength is in her tongue. She is a woman of wisdom and grace, and she reverently and worshipfully honors God.

How pleasant it is to hear this woman of grace speak in that low, soothing voice that in some respects characterizes a true lady. She never gossips, never slanders, and is never hasty with her words. She understands how often otherwise good characters are spoiled by an unbridled tongue. She is firm but gentle and recognizes that there is a time to speak and a time to be silent. She is prudent and has the law of love and kindness written upon her heart, and it is displayed in her actions.

Focused on the importance of her inner beauty, the woman of grace knows she is precious to God, not because of the clothes she wears, hairstyles, expensive jewelry, and other fancies; He delights in her gentle and quiet spirit (1 Peter 3:1–4). She is not headstrong, selfish, easily irritated, or impatient; regardless of the beauty of the exterior, these qualities are of utmost distraction. The graced woman is humble, respectful, devoted, affectionate, and patient, as she knows good things come to those who wait upon the Lord (Lam. 3:25).

There is no need to overly pursue superficial things or look to society for approval or acceptance. To "lay and play" with no commitment is not her lifestyle. She does not chase love or allow others to discount her worth. She understands that "a woman's heart should be so hidden in God that a man has to seek Him just to find her" (Max Lucado). To compete with others or put others down for self-gratification is not in her makeup. When she looks in the mirror, she looks beyond the image staring her in the face. She is pleased with herself and is at peace within herself because she is confident in who she is and Whose she is. The treasure so many women seek, the woman of grace has already discovered within her. She is God's masterpiece!

Excellence is a way of life for the woman of grace. She is elegant in her dress, skilled, industrious, a hard worker, energetic, and adored, and she allows her own works to praise her. To be found idle, lazy, slothful, sloppy, and useless are not traits ever named in describing her. She does all things well because the Greater One is in her! God is with her; therefore, she bears up under disappointments, disadvantages, and even disasters, knowing that nothing is ever impossible when He is on her side!

Above all, the woman of grace fears the Lord, which is the foundation of true wisdom. She stands in awesome respect of His power and majesty. She has sound understanding and good moral insight, as a result of following God's principles. When in trouble, she runs to Him rather than away from Him, never being ashamed, remaining confident of His unconditional love.

Today I have written about *you*, the graced woman! Every imperfection that would prevent you from becoming the graced woman has been perfected by the blood of Jesus. Put the past behind you. Today is a new day, and God has made all things new! I invite you to step into the real you—the bold, beautiful, confident, radiant, unique, highly favored woman of grace!

God said in Genesis 1, "Light in Me be...," and light came into existence. So I say to you, "Woman of grace in you, be!"

TODAY'S CONFESSION

Lord, You are my Master, and I am Your masterpiece! Every good thing I have comes from You. All that I am, and all that I can ever hope to be, I owe to You. I am happy from the inside out, and from the outside in, I am firmly formed.

Today, I decree that I am growing, changing, and evolving into the graced woman You have created me to be. I acknowledge every good thing that is in me in Christ Jesus. I am a woman of virtue. I am capable, intelligent, patient, industrious, and trustworthy. I am priceless! I am far more valuable than precious jewels. I am not rude, arrogant, or inflated with pride, nor do I act unbecomingly. When I speak, I always have something worthwhile to say, and I say it kindly. I am quick to help the poor and those in need.

I am wise in all I undertake because You are my guide. You counsel me; even at night my heart instructs me. I keep my eyes on You, and I refuse to be shaken, for You are right beside me. My body rests in safety knowing that You will never abandon me. In the midst of trials and opposition, I remain unshakeable, confident, undaunted, and certain of victory because You are with me.

I can do everything You have called me to do through Jesus, Who strengthens and empowers me. I am self-sufficient in Christ's sufficiency. I am ready for anything, I can face anything, and I am equal to anything through Jesus, Who infuses me with inner strength and confident peace.

Thank You for showing me the way of life and for granting me the joy of Your presence and the pleasure of living with You forever.

Be it unto me according to Your Word! I am the graced woman!

Psalm 16; Proverbs 31:10–31; 1 Corinthians 13:4–8; Philippians 4:13

The Graced Woman

I am the graced woman;
I walk in the unmerited favor of God.
I may stumble, and I may fall,
but in the end I stand tall.

Think about it…
Remember the time you fell
and thought you were at your lowest point…
you can look back at that now and see
that it was only a checkpoint—
Nothing broken, nothing lacking
but the gain of a new mind-set.

I am the graced woman,
not because my mother molded me into this
nor because my father raised me to think I was…
I exude excellence in every step I take.
I keep my head up so that my crown never falls.
I am a queen.
I portray a portrait of perfection,
even when everything isn't so perfect.

Why?
Because I am the graced woman
and because I am blessed with God's grace.
Even when I struggle,
my countenance never falls.
I am the graced woman...

Now say that as many times as it takes for you to believe it!

Brianna Laurielle Matthews

About the Author

Pastor Judith C. Matthews is a native of Gainesville, Florida, and is the wife of George M. Matthews II, senior pastor and founder of New Life Interfaith Ministries, Inc. They have two sons, Oscar and George III, and one daughter, Brianna.

Pastor Judith enjoys her involvement in the women's ministry and her overall administrative responsibilities at New Life. She serves as the executive director of New Life Interfaith Ministries, Inc., where she oversees the daily operation of the ministry. Pastor Judith's greatest enjoyment in life comes from studying the Word of God. The message she feels God has commissioned her to impart to the Body of Christ stems from Hosea 4:6, "My people are destroyed for lack of knowledge."

"In every area of our lives, if we are experiencing failure, it is because we have not established the Word of God in our hearts and His promises to us, the Body of Christ," she says. "Many have heard the Word but have not allowed it to take root in their lives. The Word of God takes root in our lives when we become doers, practicing and applying the Word on a daily basis. To become the 'complete woman' God has created within us requires consistent feeding on His words because they are spirit, and they are life."

Bible Abbreviations

Unless otherwise noted, all scripture quotations are from the King James Version of the Bible. The abbreviations for the versions are as follows.

American Standard Version (ASV)
Amplified Bible (AMP)
Amplified Bible, Classic Edition (AMPC)
Contemporary English Version (CEV)
Easy-to-Read Version (ERV)
English Standard Version (ESV)
GOD'S WORD Translation (GW)
Good News Translation (GNT)
Holman Christian Standard Bible (HCSB)
King James Version (KJV)
Living Bible (TLB)
The Message (MSG)
Modern English Version (MEV)
New American Standard Bible (NASB)
New International Version (NIV)
New King James Version (NKJV)
New Living Translation (NLT)

CPSIA information can be obtained
at www.ICGtesting.com
Printed in the USA
LVOW13s1257130617
537955LV00014B/445/P